FORWARD/COMMENTARY

Civil Service Retirement System (CSRS) and Federal Employees Retirement System (FERS) Handbook for Personnel and Payroll Offices

The Office of Personnel Management (OPM) is the human resources agency and personnel policy manager for the Federal Government. OPM directs human resources and employee management services, administers retirement benefits, manages healthcare and insurance programs, oversees merit-based and inclusive hiring into the civil service. This Handbook consists of 10 Volumes as follows:

VOL. I - Administrative Chapters

VOL. II - Coverage Chapters

VOL. III - Service Credit Chapter

VOL. IV - Contributions Chapters

VOL. V - Retirement Eligibility Chapters

VOL. VI - Computation of Benefits Chapters

VOL. VII - Disability Benefits Chapters

VOL. VIII - Death Benefits Chapters

VOL. IX - Record Keeping Chapters

VOL. X – Miscellaneous

Why buy a book you can download for free? We print this so you don't have to.

Some are available only in electronic media. Some online docs are missing pages or barely legible.

We at 4th Watch Publishing are former government employees, so we know how government employees actually use the handbooks. When a new handbook is released, a personnel specialist prints it out, punches holes and puts it in a 3-ring binder. While this is not a big deal for a 5 or 10-page document, many OPM documents are over 100 pages and printing a large document is a time-consuming effort. So, a personnel specialist that's paid $25 an hour is spending hours simply printing out the tools needed to do the job. That's time that could be better spent. We publish these documents so personnel specialist s can focus on what they were hired to do. It's much more cost-effective to just order the latest version from Amazon.com

Copyright © 2018 4th Watch Publishing All Rights Reserved

Check out another of our OPM books titled: "**7 OPM Handbooks**". It contains these OPM Handbooks on the following subjects:

1. Human Resources Flexibilities and Authorities in the Federal Government

2. Compensation Flexibilities to Recruit and Retain Cybersecurity Professionals

3. Handbook on Alternative Work Schedules

4. Handbook on Pay and Leave Benefits for Federal Employees Affected by Severe Weather Conditions or Other Emergency Situations

5. Negotiating Flexible and Compressed Work Schedules

6. Washington, DC, Area Dismissal and Closure Procedures

7. Handbook on Leave and Workplace Flexibilities for Childbirth, Adoption and Foster Care

Civil Service Retirement System (CSRS) and Federal Employees Retirement System (FERS)
Handbook for Personnel and Payroll Offices

VOLUME I - Administrative Chapters

C001 — Administration and General Provisions (04/1998)
C002 — Cost-of-Living Adjustments (04/1998)
C003 — Reconsideration and Appeal (04/1998)
C004 — Debt Collection (04/1998)
C005 — Court Orders (04/1998)

VOLUME II - Coverage Chapters

C010 — Coverage (07/2017)
C011 — Elections of FERS Coverage (04/1998)
C012 — Special Coverage Rules (04/1998)

VOLUME III - Service Credit Chapter

C020 — Creditable Civilian Service (04/1998)
C021 — Service Credit Payments for Civilian Service (04/1998)
C022 — Creditable Military Service (04/1998)
C023 — Service Credit Payments for Post-56 Military Service (04/1998)

VOLUME IV - Contributions Chapters

C030 — Employee Deductions and Agency Contributions 04/1998)
C031 — Voluntary Contributions (04/1998)
C032 — Refunds (04/1998)
C033 — Return of Excess Contributions (04/1998)
C034 — Designation of Beneficiary (09/2015)

VOLUME V - Retirement Eligibility Chapters

C040 — Planning and Applying for Retirement (04/1998)
C041 — Voluntary Retirement Based on Age and Service (06/2015)
C042 — MRA + 10 Retirement (04/1998)
C043 — Early Voluntary Retirement (04/1998)
C044 — Discontinued Service Retirement (04/1998)
C045 — Deferred Retirement (04/1998)
C046 — Special Retirement Provisions for Law Enforcement Officers, Firefighters, Air Traffic Controllers, and Military Reserve Technicians (04/1998)
Important Notice: Enhanced Disability and Survivor Annuity Computations

Civil Service Retirement System (CSRS) and Federal Employees Retirement System (FERS) Handbook for Personnel and Payroll Offices

VOLUME VI - Computation of Benefits Chapters

C050 — Computation of Annuity Under the General Formula (04/1998)
C051 — Retiree Annuity Supplement (04/1998)
C052 — Survivor Elections (04/1998)
C053 — Alternative Annuity Elections (04/1998)
C054 — Special Computation Formulas for Law Enforcement Officers, Firefighters, and Air Traffic Controllers (04/1998)
C055 — Computation for Part-Time Employees (04/1998)

VOLUME VII - Disability Benefits Chapters

C060 — Disability Retirement (04/1998)
C061 — Computation of Disability Retirement Benefits (04/1998)
Important Notice: Enhanced Disability and Survivor Annuity Computations

VOLUME VIII - Death Benefits Chapters

C070 — Spouse Benefits - Death of an Employee (04/1998)
Important Notice: Enhanced Disability and Survivor Annuity Computations
C071 — Spouse Benefits - Death of an Annuitant (04/1998)
C072 — Spouse Benefits - Death of a Former Employee (04/1998)
C073 — Children's Benefits (04/1998)
C074 — Former Spouse Survivor Benefits (04/1998)
C075 — Lump Sum Benefits (04/1998)

VOLUME IX - Record Keeping Chapters

C080 — Payroll Office Reporting of Deductions and Contributions (04/1998)
C081 — Individual Retirement Records and Registers of Separations and Transfers (04/1998)
C082 — (Reserved)   (04/1998)
C083 — Self-Evaluation Guide for Agency Administration of Employee Benefit Programs (04/1998)
C084 — Correction of Retirement Records (04/1998)
C085 — Headcounts (04/1998)

VOLUME X – Miscellaneous

C100 — Reemployed Annuitants   (10/2013)
C101 — Special Retirement Provisions for Senior Officials (04/1998)
C102 — Relationship Between Retirement Annuity and Compensation for Work-Related Injuries and Diseases   (10/2013)

Table of Contents

Subchapter 1A General Information

Section 1A1.1-1 Overview ... 1
- A. Introduction ... 1
- B. Topics Covered ... 1
- C. Organization of Subchapter ... 1
- D. Statement of Authority ... 1

Section 1A1.1-2 Civil Service Retirement System ... 2
- A. Type of System ... 2
- B. Benefits ... 2
- C. Contributions ... 2
- D. Voluntary Contributions ... 2
- E. Thrift Savings Plan ... 2
- F. CSRS Offset Contributions ... 3
- G. CSRS Offset Benefit ... 3

Section 1A1.1-3 Federal Employees Retirement System ... 4
- A. General ... 4
- B. Social Security ... 4
- C. Basic FERS Annuity ... 4
- D. Thrift Savings Plan ... 4

Subchapter 1B About this Handbook

Part 1B1 Overview

Section 1B1.1-1 Overview ... 5
- A. Introduction ... 5
- B. Topics Covered ... 5
- C. Organization of Subchapter ... 5
- D. Statement of Authority ... 5

Part 1B2 Organization

Section 1B2.1-1 Presentation of Information 6
   A. Format 6
   B. Structure 6
   C. Logos 6

Section 1B2.1-2 Subdivisions 7
   A. Chapters 7
   B. Subchapters 7
   C. Parts and Subparts 7
   D. Sections 8
   E. Paragraphs 8

Part 1B3 Subscriptions

Section 1B3.1-1 How to Obtain the Handbook 9
   A. The "Rider" 9
   B. Direct Orders 9
   C. Downloading from the Bulletin Board 9
   D. Distribution Within Agencies 10
   E. Non-Federal Entities 10

Subchapter 1C OPM and Agency Responsibilities

Part 1C1 Overview

Section 1C1.1-1 Overview 11
   A. Introduction 11
   B. Topics Covered 11
   C. Organization of Subchapter 11
   D. Statement of Authority 11

CSRS Administration and General Provisions FERS
Chapter 1

Part 1C2 OPM Responsibilities

Section 1C2.1-1 OPM Responsibilities 12
   A.   Administration of CSRS and FERS 12
   B.   Regulations and Instructions 12
   C.   Individual Retirement Record 12
   D.   Claims Adjudication 12
   E.   Account Maintenance 13
   F.   Financial Records 14
   G.   Continuing System Administration 14
   H.   Retirement and Insurance Service 14

Part 1C3 Agency Responsibilities

Section 1C3.1-1 Agency Responsibilities 15
   A.   Agency Head 15
   B.   Agency Retirement Counselor 15
   C.   Local Personnel Offices 16
   D.   Payroll Offices 17

Subchapter 1D Job Aids

Section 1D1.1-1 Copies of Job Aids 19
   A.   Description 19

Agency Retirement Counselor Responsibilities 20

   1.   Management 20
   2.   Resources 21
   3.   Policy Development and Interpretation 21
   4.   Resources 22
   5.   Training and Education 22
   6.   Resources 22
   7.   Evaluation 22
   8.   Resources 23
   9.   Duties Not Normally Performed by a Retirement Counselor 23

CSRS — Administration and General Provisions — FERS
Chapter 1

Subchapter 1A General Information

Section 1A1.1-1 Overview

A. Introduction

This Chapter briefly describes the organization and use of this Handbook, the "CSRS and FERS Handbook for Personnel and Payroll Offices." The Handbook contains the instructions agency personnel and payroll offices need to carry out their responsibilities for basic benefits under the Civil Service Retirement System (CSRS) and the Federal Employees Retirement System (FERS). This Chapter also describes the responsibilities of the Office of Personnel Management (OPM) and employing agencies in retirement matters. This Handbook is issued as CSRS and FERS Handbook for Personnel and Payroll Offices. It replaces FPM Supplement 830-1 and FPM Supplement 831-1, Retirement.

B. Topics Covered

This subchapter contains:

- A brief description of the CSRS; and

- A brief description of the FERS.

C. Organization of Subchapter

This subchapter has three sections.

Section	Name of Section	Page
1A1.1-1	Overview	1
1A1.1-2	Civil Service Retirement System	2
1A1.1-3	Federal Employees Retirement System	4

D. Statement of Authority

This Handbook is based on the laws and regulations cited below.

- United States Code: Chapters 83 and 84

- Code of Federal Regulations: Parts 831, 841, 842, 843, 844, 845, and 846.12

Section 1A1.1-2 Civil Service Retirement System

A.	**Type of System**	The Civil Service Retirement System (CSRS) is a defined benefit, contributory retirement system. Employees share in the expense of the annuities to which they become entitled.
B.	**Benefits**	CSRS benefits are based on the employee's "high-3" average pay and the years of service. Under the general formula, 30 years of service provide 56.25 percent of the "high-3" average salary.
C.	**Contributions**	CSRS covered employees contribute 7, 7 1/2 or 8 percent of pay to CSRS and, while they generally pay no Social Security retirement, survivor and disability (OASDI) tax, they must pay the Medicare tax (currently 1.45 percent of pay). The employing agency matches the employee's CSRS contributions.
D.	**Voluntary Contributions**	Employees may contribute up to 10 percent of the basic pay for their creditable service to a voluntary contribution account. Accounts earn a market rate of interest. The employee may withdraw the funds from the account at any time or use them to purchase an additional annuity at retirement. The additional annuity is $7 a year for each $100 in the account, plus 20¢ for each full year the person is over age 55 at retirement.
E.	**Thrift Savings Plan**	Employees may contribute up to 5 percent of pay to the Thrift Savings Plan (see section 1A1.1-3D). There is no Government contribution.

Section 1A1.1-2 Civil Service Retirement System (Cont.)

F.	**CSRS Offset Contributions**	CSRS-Offset covered employees are covered by Social Security coverage because they were separated from CSRS covered Federal employment for more than a year and returned to a position in which they were covered by CSRS after 1983. For these employees, their OASDI withholdings are offset from their CSRS contributions, so that the combined Social Security and CSRS contributions are the same as for employees who have CSRS coverage only.
G.	**CSRS Offset Benefit**	When CSRS Offset employees retire, they receive full CSRS benefits until they are eligible for Social Security benefits, generally at age 62. At that time, the CSRS benefit is offset by the portion of their Social Security benefit that represents the period of time they were covered by both CSRS and Social Security.

Section 1A1.1-3 Federal Employees Retirement System

A. General

The Federal Employees Retirement System (FERS) is a three-tiered plan consisting of Social Security, a basic FERS annuity, and the Thrift Savings Plan.

B. Social Security

Employees under FERS are covered by full Social Security taxes. The Social Security tax for 1998 is 7.65 percent of pay (6.2 percent for retirement and 1.45 percent for Medicare). Annual earnings in excess of the maximum taxable wage base > ($68,400 in 1998) < are not subject to the Social Security tax. See the Social Security Administration's "Social Security Handbook" for more information.

C. Basic FERS Annuity

The basic FERS annuity is based on the employee's length of service and the "high-3" average pay. For most employees, the formula for computing the annual annuity is 1 percent of average pay for each year of creditable service.

Employees contribute 0.8 percent of pay to FERS for the basic benefit.

D. Thrift Savings Plan

Employees may contribute up to 10 percent of their pay to the Thrift Savings Plan. These contributions are tax-deferred. The Government contributes 1 percent of pay and matches a portion of the employee's contributions. The maximum Government contribution is 5 percent of pay. The Thrift Savings Plan is administered by the Federal Retirement Thrift Investment Board. See their publication "Summary of Thrift Savings Plan for Federal Employees" for more information.

Subchapter 1B About this Handbook
Part 1B1 Overview

Section 1B1.1-1 Overview

A. Introduction	This subchapter provides information about the "CSRS and FERS Handbook for Personnel and Payroll Offices." It explains how the information is presented, describes the subdivisions of the Handbook, and gives information about how to obtain the Handbook.
B. Topics Covered	This subchapter contains: • An explanation of how information is presented; • A description of the subdivisions of the Handbook; and • Information about how to obtain the Handbook.
C. Organization of Subchapter	This subchapter has three parts with a total of four sections.

Section	Name of Part	Name of Section	Page
1B1.1-1	Overview	Overview	5
1B2.1-1	Organization	Presentation of Information	6
1B2.1-2		Subdivisions	7
1B3.1-1	Subscriptions	How to Obtain the Handbook	9

D. Statement of Authority	This subchapter is based on the laws and regulations cited below. • United States Code: Title 5, Chapters 83 and 84 • Code of Federal Regulations: Title 5, Parts 831, 841, 842, 843, 844, 845, and 846

Part 1B2 Organization

Section 1B2.1-1 Presentation of Information

A. Format

The information in this Handbook is presented in a format that is somewhat different from most OPM publications. The information is subdivided as follows:

- Chapters
- Subchapters
- Parts
- Subparts
- Sections
- Paragraphs

See section 1B2.1-2 below for an explanation of these subdivisions.

B. Structure

Most Chapters in this Handbook have as their first two subchapters, a subchapter on the Civil Service Retirement System (CSRS) and a subchapter on the Federal Employees Retirement System (FERS). The CSRS subchapter gives complete information about the Chapter subject and how it pertains to CSRS. The FERS subchapter states what CSRS information also applies for FERS and contains the information that is different for FERS.

EXCEPTION: In some Chapters, (such as this Chapter and the coverage Chapter) the CSRS and FERS information is merged into a single subchapter.

C. Logos

Subchapters containing CSRS information have a CSRS logo at the top of the page. Subchapters containing FERS information have a FERS logo. Subchapters containing information that applies to both systems have both logos. This lets readers tell at a glance whether a page contains CSRS information, FERS information, or both.

Section 1B2.1-2 Subdivisions

A. **Chapters** Chapters are the major subdivisions of this Handbook. Each Chapter is identified with a number and a title.

Example: Chapter 10 Coverage

B. **Subchapters** Chapters are divided into subchapters. Subchapter topics are limited to specific categories-CSRS, FERS, Examples, Charts, Illustrations, and Forms Facsimiles for Local Reproduction. In some Chapters the last three items are combined as "Job Aids." Each subchapter has a title and is identified with a capital letter that follows the Chapter number.

Example: Subchapter 10B   Examples of Application of Coverage Rules

C. **Parts and Subparts** Subchapters may be divided into parts and subparts, but not all subchapters have them. Parts and subparts are primarily to group sections into coherent units. Each part has a title and is identified with a number following the Chapter and subchapter identifiers. To identify a subpart, the Handbook system places a period (.) after the part identifier, followed by a number.

Example of a part identifier:

   Part 10B1   New Hires

Example of a subpart identifier:

   Subpart 10A1.2   Historical Background

Section 1B2.1-2 Subdivisions (Cont.)

D. Sections Sections are the basic informational units of this Handbook. A subchapter may have no parts or subparts, but it always has sections. Each section has a number preceded by all the identifiers for the subpart and a dash. (If there is no part or subpart, the identifier for the missing subdivision is 1.)

Example: **Section 10A1.2-1 Background: Retirement System Coverage**

This numbering system allows users to locate any section in the Handbook by its number without needing to consult an index or table of contents.

E. Paragraphs Sections are organized in paragraphs. Each paragraph has a label appearing in bold type to its left and identified by a capital letter (for example, A). Paragraphs may be made of narrative information, charts, lists, or any other device that lends itself to clear presentation of the information.

CSRS — Administration and General Provisions — FERS
Chapter 1

Part 1B3 Subscriptions

Section 1B3.1-1 How to Obtain the Handbook

A. The "Rider"
OPM periodically notifies agencies of the opportunity to purchase publications, including this Handbook, through the rider system. By purchasing the Handbook through the rider system, agencies receive the advantage of bulk printing rates. Agencies that subscribe through the rider system automatically receive new updates of the Handbook, but would not receive previously published updates. As with other orders through the rider system, orders for the Handbook must be submitted from the agency headquarters level.

B. Direct Orders
The Washington, DC, Headquarters Printing Office of Federal agencies, and non-Federal entities, may place orders with:

> U.S. Government Printing Office
> Superintendent of Documents
> Washington, DC 20402

Orders can be placed any time with GPO. The subscription includes material published to date and updates as they are issued.

C. Downloading from OPM's Web site and the Bulletin Board
The Handbook also is available on OPM's Web site at www.opm.gov/asd/htm/hod.htm and on OPM ONLINE, the OPM computer bulletin board.

The telephone number for OPM ONLINE is 202-606-4800. Your communications software should be set to the following:

> Baud: Up to 14,400
> Parity: None
> Data bits: 8
> Stop bit: 1

Section 1B3.1-1 How to Obtain the Handbook (Cont.)

C.	**Downloading from the Bulletin Board (Cont.)**	The information is available from the main menu. Follow the instructions below.

Select:

    (1) Forums: Area of Special Interest
              then
    (A) Retirement and Insurance Service
              then
    (A) For Benefits Administration
              then
Look for your particular interest |
| D. | **Distribution Within Agencies** | The extent of the distribution of the Handbook within an agency is a matter for the determination of the agency. Employing offices must follow internal agency procedures to obtain sufficient number of copies of the Handbook to meet their needs.

When updates are either received in incorrect quantities or not received at all, you should contact your agency's Printing Officer. The Printing Officer will contact the agency's GPO Account Representative. To find out who your agency's Printing Officer is, contact your administrative services personnel at agency headquarters. |
| E. | **Non-Federal Entities** | Private persons and organizations may subscribe to this Handbook by contacting the Government Printing Office directly. |

Subchapter 1C OPM and Agency Responsibilities
Part 1C1 Overview

Section 1C1.1-1 Overview

A. Introduction

This subchapter covers the respective responsibilities of OPM and employing agencies for retirement matters.

B. Topics Covered

This subchapter covers:

- OPM's responsibilities for administering CSRS and FERS;

- General agency responsibilities for retirement matters;

- The responsibilities of the agency headquarters level Retirement Counselor as the agency's program manager for retirement;

- The responsibilities of retirement counselors in local installations; and

- The responsibilities of payroll offices.

C. Organization of Subchapter

This subchapter has three parts.

Part	Name of Part	Page
1C1.1-1	Overview	11
1C2.1-1	OPM Responsibilities	12
1C3.1-1	Agency Responsibilities	15

D. Statement of Authority

This subchapter is based on the laws and regulations cited below.

- United States Code: 5 U.S.C. 8350

- Code of Federal Regulations: 5 CFR 831.102 and Part 841

Part 1C2 OPM Responsibilities

Section 1C2.1-1 OPM Responsibilities

A.	**Administration of CSRS and FERS**	OPM has overall responsibility for administering the CSRS and FERS. Its major responsibilities are outlined below.
B.	**Regulations and Instructions**	OPM issues regulations and instructions to administer the retirement systems. The retirement regulations are published in Parts 831 (for CSRS) and 841 through 846 (for FERS) of Title 5, Code of Federal Regulations. Implementing instructions are published in this Handbook.
C.	**Individual Retirement Record**	OPM maintains individual retirement records of separated employees, and prior records of employees who have transferred between agencies. OPM also maintains CSRS designations of beneficiary on active and separated employees and FERS designations of beneficiary of separated employees and annuitants.
D.	**Claims Adjudication**	OPM responsibilities for claims adjudication include the following activities.

- OPM receives retirement packages from agency payroll offices and adjudicates CSRS and FERS retirement and survivor claims, as well as applications for refunds of retirement monies and for service credit payments for civilian service.

- In adjudicating claims for retirement, OPM's benefits specialists review all documents to verify entitlement to annuity, health benefits coverage, and life insurance coverage and, if necessary, obtain additional documentation. The specialists determine benefit entitlement under the applicable provisions of law, coordinate benefit entitlement as required with Social Security, OWCP, etc., and authorize payment of annuity.

Section 1C2.1-1 OPM Responsibilities (Cont.)

D. Claims Adjudication (Cont.)

- In adjudicating claims for death benefits, OPM determines survivors' eligibility for benefits and the type of benefit due.

- OPM determines applicants' eligibility for refunds of retirement deductions and authorizes payment of refunds. OPM also determines applicants' eligibility to make deposits and redeposits for service, confirms creditability of service for retirement, and computes the amount due the Civil Service Retirement and Disability Fund (the Fund).

- In carrying out its responsibilities for claims adjudication, OPM must also apply pertinent provisions of law requiring payment of benefits to former spouses of employees and retirees, collection of debts owed the U.S. Government, collection of Federal and State income taxes, and collections of overpayments from the Fund.

E. Account Maintenance

OPM serves as "personnel and payroll office" for approximately 2 million retirees and survivors. In this capacity, OPM carries out activities such as the following.

- OPM redetermines benefits when agencies submit additional information about an employee's employment history, or when events, such as a post-retirement change in marital or family status, change a retiree's or survivor's entitlement.

- OPM conducts the Federal Employees Health Benefits (FEHB) open season activities for annuitants and survivors.

- OPM responds to inquiries from annuitants and maintains annuitant accounts when they move, change tax withholdings, or health benefits and life insurance, etc.

- OPM carries out various survey and matching programs to verify annuitants' continued entitlement to benefits.

Section 1C2.1-1 OPM Responsibilities (Cont.)

F.	**Financial Records**	OPM accounts for retirement monies received by OPM and disbursed to benefit recipients, insurance carriers, and Federal and State tax entities, maintains retirement control accounts, and determines the financial condition of the Fund.
G.	**Continuing System Administration**	OPM prepares forms and informational materials for use by employees, agencies, and annuitants, provides training for agency personnel, responds to inquiries from agency headquarters Retirement Counselors, and makes recommendations to the President and Congress for changes to improve the retirement system.
H.	**Retirement and Insurance Service**	OPM's Retirement and Insurance Service (RIS) carries out the agency's responsibilities for administering CSRS and FERS.

CSRS — Administration and General Provisions — Chapter 1 — FERS   15

Part 1C3 Agency Responsibilities

Section 1C3.1-1 Agency Responsibilities

A. Agency Head

1. An agency head or his or her designee is responsible for designating the agency headquarters level Retirement Counselor and designating certifying officers. Agencies should notify OPM in writing of any change in the designated Retirement Counselor. The notification should come from the Director of Personnel or equivalent official, to the Agency Services Division.

2. The agency head also bears overall responsibility for the quality and timeliness of submissions of records to OPM. Agencies are responsible for insuring that all records and required documentation are received by OPM no later than 30 days after the date of separation (or death in the case of a deceased employee). For disability retirements, agencies are to ensure that all records and supporting documentation will be received by OPM no later than 30 days after the date on which the employee files the application with the employing agency.

B. Agency Retirement Counselor

1. The agency headquarters level Retirement Counselor is the agency headquarters level program manager for retirement matters. The agency Retirement Counselor responsibilities include:

   - Managing retirement program matters within the agency;

   - Serving as the agency liaison with OPM and other agencies on retirement matters;

   - Interpreting policy directives, reviewing and commenting on proposed policy changes affecting government-wide programs, formulating agency policy and seeking assistance from OPM if needed to resolve questions not addressed in OPM's written instructions;

   - Providing for training and education of local personnel who are responsible for retirement matters, and for employee counseling programs; and

Section 1C3.1-1 Agency Responsibilities (Cont.)

B. Agency Retirement Counselor (Cont.)

- Evaluating the accuracy and timeliness of retirement submissions to OPM and the effectiveness of agency pre-retirement counseling programs, and making recommendations to agency management.

2. An agency retirement counselor **does not** normally:

- Provide one-on-one retirement counseling to employees; or

- Become involved in individual retirement cases.

3. Subchapter 1D contains a more detailed description of agency retirement counselor responsibilities for agency use in agency retirement counselors' position descriptions

C. Local Personnel Offices

At the local level, agencies are responsible for:

- Determining employees' retirement coverage correctly;

- Providing pre-retirement counseling for groups of employees and individual employees;

- Counseling employees concerning making service credit payments and post-56 military deposits and assisting employees with applications;

- Verifying creditability of service;

- Verifying retirees' eligibility to retain health and life insurance in retirement, certifying life insurance coverage and amounts in death in service cases, and transferring necessary documentation of health and life insurance coverage to OPM;

- Providing employees and survivors of deceased employees estimates of expected benefits and assisting them in the preparation of the retirement or refund application and related documentation;

Section 1C3.1-1 Agency Responsibilities (Cont.)

C. Local Personnel Offices (Cont.)

- Certifying the personnel office portion of applications for retirement, refunds, death benefits, and service credit payments;

- Directing annuitants and their survivors and other former employees who have questions about their benefits to OPM for assistance; and

- Requesting assistance, as needed, from the agency headquarters Retirement Counselor about retirement matters.

For a complete discussion of agency responsibilities in assisting employees to plan for retirement and apply for annuity, see Chapter 40, Planning and Applying for Retirement.

D. Payroll Offices

Agency payroll offices are responsible for:

- Withholding retirement deductions from employees' pay, making the correct agency contribution, and transmitting these monies to the Fund;

- Preparing and maintaining an individual retirement record for each employee who is covered by CSRS or FERS;

- Maintaining post-56 military deposit accounts;

- Certifying individual retirement records and related records, and ensuring the correctness of data in these records;

- Certifying that the payroll office portion of applications for retirement and survivor benefits is accurate and complete; and

- Maintaining retirement control accounts and preparing retirement accounting reports.

BLANK PAGE

CSRS Administration and General Provisions Chapter 1 FERS

Subchapter 1D Job Aids

Section 1D1.1-1 Copies of Job Aids

A. Description	• This subchapter contains the following job aid for agency use: Description of Agency Retirement Counselor Responsibilities

Agency Retirement Counselor Responsibilities

The agency headquarters Retirement Counselor is responsible for establishing and coordinating department/agency retirement policy and efficient retirement processing procedures, and assuring policy compliance among the various operating offices.

These activities involve functioning as liaison within the department/agency between payroll and personnel offices and, in large departments, between the central policy-making branch and operating personnel offices. In carrying out external liaison activities with other agencies, primarily OPM, the Retirement Counselor will be an active member of the Interagency Advisory Group of Retirement Counselors attending meetings and participating in subcommittees.

The combination of extensive knowledge of Federal retirement systems and of department/agency operations uniquely qualifies the Retirement Counselor to formulate and provide input to retirement policy at the department/agency level and to respond as the department/agency spokesperson when asked for input on retirement matters.

The Retirement Counselor is also responsible for assuring that employees are able to make informed decisions regarding their retirement benefits. This may best be accomplished via a comprehensive retirement counseling program including on-demand counseling by trained, knowledgeable personnelists, and regularly scheduled pre-retirement seminars. If such a program is already in existence, the Retirement Counselor will be involved in evaluating its effectiveness and instituting enhancements where necessary. If no program exists, it may be necessary to develop a retirement counseling policy and implement a program.

In carrying out these responsibilities, a Retirement Counselor is typically engaged in the following activities:

1. **Management** Oversees and provides direction to the department/agency retirement counseling program.

    Serves as central point for the dissemination of policy and procedural guidance to appropriate headquarters and field operating personnel offices.

    Serves as the authoritative resource in department/agency for technical information regarding retirement matters.

Agency Retirement Counselor Responsibilities (Cont.)

1. **Management (Cont.)**

   Serves as departmental/agency liaison with OPM and other agencies on retirement matters.

   Manages a communication network within the department/agency of retirement counselors and processors, and coordinates the flow of information between them and external agencies (OPM, SSA, IRS, Thrift Board).

   Coordinates retirement processing and policy issues among internal offices such as payroll, classification, staffing, etc.

   Regularly exchanges information with OPM regarding retirement-related issues, including legislative and regulatory activity, and court cases.

2. **Resources**

   Up-to-date copies of OPM publications, including technical and processing manuals.

   Access to knowledgeable sources at OPM.

   Regular IAG meetings.

   Special training.

3. **Policy Development and Interpretation**

   Formulates departmental/agency policy and provides overall direction and guidance on retirement matters.

   Reviews and comments on proposed legislation and regulations affecting government-wide benefits programs.

   Interprets policy, regulations, and legislation, and develops department/agency operating procedures.

Agency Retirement Counselor Responsibilities (Cont.)

4.	**Resources**	Timely receipt of proposed, interim, and final regulations from OPM.
		Advance consultation with OPM when possible about upcoming changes that may significantly impact department/agency operations.
5.	**Training and Education**	Provides training to headquarters and field retirement counselors and processors through in-house or external sources.
		Provides for the delivery of pre-retirement seminars and counseling to employees through in-house or external sources.
		Publicizes changes in retirement benefits, open season deadlines, etc., through in-house publications such as employee memos and newsletters.
6.	**Resources**	Up-to-date information about interagency training resources.
		Information exchange about courses and materials available from external sources.
		Timely receipt of information suitable for publication.
7.	**Evaluation**	Conducts evaluations of operating personnel office responsibilities, such as coverage decisions, retirement coding, and quality and timeliness of agency submissions of retirement documents to OPM, and takes appropriate steps to improve performance where needed.
		Evaluates the effectiveness of department/agency-wide pre-retirement counseling programs and takes appropriate steps to improve their quality as needed.

Agency Retirement Counselor Responsibilities (Cont.)

8.	**Resources**	OPM-developed criteria for measuring acceptable performance in operating programs.
		Basic pre-retirement counseling program standards and criteria to be used when expanding a program.
9.	**Duties Not Normally Performed by a Retirement Counselor**	Does not function as an expediter of retirement cases at OPM except in extraordinary situations.
		Does not provide one-on-one retirement counseling to employees. However, Retirement Counselors at very small agencies may also be responsible for providing counseling services.

| *CSRS* | Cost-of-Living Adjustments
Chapter 2 | *FERS* i |

Table of Contents

Subchapter 2A CSRS

Part 2A1 General Information

Section 2A1.1-1 Overview 1
  A. Introduction 1
  B. Topics Covered 1
  C. Organization of Subchapter 1
  D. Statement of Authority 1

Section 2A1.1-2 Definitions 2
  A. Base Quarter 2
  B. Consumer Price Index (CPI) 2
  C. Base Quarter Price Index 2
  D. Cost-Of-Living Adjustment (COLA) 2
  E. Effective Date 2
  F. Annuity Commencing Date 2

Part 2A2 Computation

Section 2A2.1-1 Computation of COLA'S 3
  A. COLA Rate 3
  B. COLA Increase 3

Part 2A3 Proration

Section 2A3.1-1 Proration of First COLA 5
  A. General Rule 5
  B. Procedure 5

Part 2A4 Survivor Annuities

Section 2A4.1-1 Survivor Annuities 7
  A. Spouse, Former Spouse, Insurable Interest 7
  B. Children 7

Part 2A5 Miscellaneous

Section 2A5.1-1 Miscellaneous Provisions 8
  A. Voluntary Contributions 8
  B. Reemployed Annuitants 8
  C. COLA Cap 8

Subchapter 2B FERS

Part 2B1 General Information

Section 2B1.1-1 Overview 9
  A. Introduction 9
  B. Organization of Subchapter 9
  C. Applicable CSRS Provision 9
  D. Statement of Authority 9

Part 2B2 Computation

Section 2B2.1-1 Computation of COLA'S 10
  A. Eligibility 10
  B. COLA Rate 11
  C. COLA Increase 12
  D. Disability Annuitants 12

Part 2B3 Proration

Section 2B3.1-1 Proration of First COLA 13
  A. General Rule 13

Part 2B4 Transfer Employees With a CSRS Component

Section 2B4.1-1 Transfer Employees with a CSRS Component 14
  A. Transfer Employees With a CSRS Component 14

Part 2B5 Survivor Annuities and Death Benefit

Section 2B5.1-1 Survivor Annuities 15
  A. Spouse, Former Spouse, Insurable Interest 15
  B. Children 15

Section 2B5.1-2 Death Benefit 16
  A. Lump-Sum Death Benefit 16

Part 2B6 Miscellaneous

Section 2B6.1-1 Miscellaneous COLA Provisions 17
  A. Disability Annuitants 17
  B. Reemployed Annuitants 17

Subchapter 2C Job Aids

Section 2C1.1-1 Copies of Job Aids 19
  Table of CSRS COLA's for Federal Retirees 19
  Table of FERS COLA's for Federal Retirees 20
  Table of COLA Adjustments to $15,000 Portion of FERS
     Basic Employee Death Benefit 21

CSRS Cost-of-Living Adjustments
Chapter 2

Subchapter 2A CSRS
Part 2A1 General Information

Section 2A1.1-1 Overview

A. Introduction	This subchapter covers CSRS annuity cost-of-living adjustments (COLA's) based on increases in the Consumer Price Index (CPI).
B. Topics Covered	This subchapter covers: • The definition of COLA's and terms related to COLA's; • The computation of COLA's; • The proration of the initial COLA; and • Additional information associated with COLA's.
C. Organization of Subchapter	The CSRS subchapter has five parts.

Part	Name of Part	Page
2A1	General Information	1
2A2	Computation	3
2A3	Proration	5
2A4	Survivor Annuities	7
2A5	Miscellaneous	8

NOTE: Subchapter 2B about COLA's for annuitants under FERS begins on page 9.

D. Statement of Authority	This subchapter is based on the laws and regulations cited below. • United States Code: 5 U.S.C. 8340 • Code of Federal Regulations: 5 CFR Part 831

CSRS Cost-of-Living Adjustments
Chapter 2

Section 2A1.1-2 Definitions

A.	**Base Quarter**	The calendar quarter ending September 30 for any given year.
B.	**Consumer Price Index (CPI)**	The index published monthly by the Department of Labor that reflects changes in consumer prices for urban wage earners and clerical workers.
C.	**Base Quarter Price Index**	The arithmetical mean of the CPI for the 3 months comprising a base quarter (currently, July, August, and September).
D.	**Cost-Of-Living Adjustment (COLA)**	An increase in an annuity based on the increase in the CPI between two consecutive base quarters.
E.	**Effective Date**	Cost-of-living adjustments are effective on December 1 of the year in which an annuitant becomes eligible. (Increases are first reflected in annuity checks payable in January following the effective date.)
F.	**Annuity Commencing Date**	The date an annuity first begins to accrue.

CSRS Cost-of-Living Adjustments — Chapter 2

Part 2A2 Computation

Section 2A2.1-1 Computation of COLA'S

A. COLA Rate

The amount of a COLA is determined by the percent change in the base quarter price index from the previous year to the year in which the COLA is to become effective, adjusted to the nearest 1/10 of 1 percent.

EXAMPLE:

Year	Base Quarter Price Index
1988	177.8
1987	113.3
Difference	4.5

$$\frac{4.5}{113.3} \times 100 = 3.97$$

COLA rate = 4.0% (adjusted to the nearest 1/10 of 1%) effective December 1, 1988

B. COLA Increase

1. An individual's new gross monthly annuity, reflecting the COLA increase, is calculated by multiplying the old gross monthly annuity by the COLA factor (1 plus the COLA rate):

    Gross monthly annuity x (1 + rate).

2. The gross monthly annuity is the annuity payable after adjustments have been made, when applicable, for all of the following:

    - Reduction for survivor benefits;

    - Reduction for alternative annuity;

    - Reduction for early retirement;

    - Reduction for unpaid deposit service performed before October 1, 1982; and

    > • Reduction for unpaid redeposit for service ended prior to October 1, 1990 <

Section 2A2.1-1 Computation of COLA'S (Cont.)

B. COLA Increase (Cont.)

EXAMPLE:

COLA = 4.0%

Gross monthly annuity before COLA	$1,730.00
Multiply by COLA factor (1 + .04)	x 1.04
Gross monthly annuity after COLA (rounded to next lower dollar)	$1,799.00

NOTE 1:   The gross monthly annuity is always rounded to the next lower dollar. However, the gross monthly annuity after a COLA must reflect an increase of at least $1.00.

NOTE 2:   The COLA is applied before withholdings are made for tax and for health and life insurance premiums.

CSRS Cost-of-Living Adjustments
Chapter 2

Part 2A3 Proration

Section 2A3.1-1 Proration of First COLA

A. General Rule

The amount of an annuitant's first COLA is prorated. The proration is based on the number of months from the annuity commencement date to the effective date of the first COLA after the commencement date.

1. Retirees receive one-twelfth of the applicable cost-of-living increase for each month, not to exceed 12 months, that they are in receipt of an annuity before December 1.

2. To receive the full December 1 increase, a retiree's commencing date for retirement can be no later than December 31 of the previous year.

B. Procedure

From the chart below, determine the number of months on the annuity roll at the time of the COLA. Divide the COLA rate by 12, and multiply the answer by the number of months on the annuity roll. Round the answer to the nearest 1/10 of 1 percent. The result is the prorated COLA.

$$\frac{\text{COLA rate}}{12} \times \text{Number of months on annuity roll} = \text{Prorated COLA}$$

If Monthly Annuity Commences During --	Number of Months On Roll is --
December of previous year	12
January	11
February	10
March	9
April	8
May	7
June	6
July	5
August	4
September	3
October	2
November	1

Section 2A3.1-1 Proration of First COLA (Cont.)

B. Procedure (Cont.) EXAMPLE 1: If a retiree's commencing date is December 1, 1989, the retiree does not receive a COLA increase in the January 1990 check but does receive the full December 1990 COLA increase in the January 1991 annuity check.

EXAMPLE 2: COLA = 4.0%

Annuity commences August 1
Number of months on roll = 4

Gross monthly annuity BEFORE COLA = $2,000

$$\frac{4}{12} \times 4 = 1.3\% \text{ Prorated COLA}$$

Gross monthly annuity AFTER COLA:
$2,000 x (1 + .013) = $2,026

IMPORTANT: The proration applies only to the annuitant's first COLA.

CSRS Cost-of-Living Adjustments Chapter 2

Part 2A4 Survivor Annuities

Section 2A4.1-1 Survivor Annuities

A. Spouse, Former Spouse, Insurable Interest

An annuity payable to an annuitant's survivor normally commences on the day after death.

1. If the retiree received his or her first COLA, the survivor annuity is not subject to proration.

2. If the retiree had not received his or her first COLA, the survivor's first COLA is prorated based on the commencing date of the retiree's annuity.

3. The proration rules also apply to the first COLA paid to the survivor of an employee who died in service.

Here are two examples that illustrate the rules listed above.

	If Employee Retires	Then Dies	Survivor COLA Is
EXAMPLE 1:	June 1	July 14	Subject to proration
EXAMPLE 2:	June 1	January 10	Not subject to proration with the next COLA increase. (Retiree received prorated increase effective December 1 following commencement of the annuity.)

NOTE: While the retiree is living, the potential survivor benefit receives the same COLA increases the annuitant receives.

B. Children

Children's annuities are increased by COLA's effective December 1 and are payable in the January annuity check. However, unlike other annuitants' COLA's, children's COLA's are not subject to proration.

The COLA is based on the annuity payable before any deductions are made (for example, health benefits).

Part 2A5 Miscellaneous

Section 2A5.1-1 Miscellaneous Provisions

A. Voluntary Contributions	The law does not provide for COLA's for additional annuities purchased at retirement by voluntary contributions.
B. Reemployed Annuitants	A reemployed annuitant's pay is offset by the amount of the annuity (see Chapter 100, Reemployed Annuitants). When a COLA is applied to the annuity, the employing office must make an additional salary offset. The agency determines the new monthly rate to be used for reducing the salary by adding the COLA (full or prorated, as appropriate) to the previous rate. The additional offset in pay is effective from December 1 of such year.
C. COLA Cap	An annuity may not be increased by a COLA to an amount that exceeds the greater of: • The current payable rate for GS-15, step 10; or • An amount equal to an individual's final pay (or average pay, if higher) increased by all cumulative average GS pay increases from the commencing date of the annuity to the effective date of the COLA. The cumulative GS increases are used in all cases, even though the individual may have been employed under a different pay system. This cap applies to any COLA increases to an annuity. In no instance is an annuity that exceeds the cap reduced.

Cost-of-Living Adjustments
Chapter 2

FERS

Subchapter 2B FERS
Part 2B1 General Information

Section 2B1.1-1 Overview

A. Introduction

This subchapter covers FERS annuity cost-of-living adjustments (COLA's) based on increases in the Consumer Price Index (CPI).

This subchapter explains how FERS differs from CSRS. It refers readers to the CSRS rule that applies or gives the FERS rule if it is different.

Subchapter 2B also provides information regarding the determination of COLA's for transfer employees with a CSRS component.

B. Organization of Subchapter

This FERS subchapter has six parts.

Part	Name of Part	Page
2B1	General Information	9
2B2	Computation	10
2B3	Proration	13
2B4	Transfer Employees With a CSRS Component	14
2B5	Survivor Annuities and Death Benefit	15
2B6	Miscellaneous	17

C. Applicable CSRS Provision

The following section of subchapter 2A applies to FERS employees:

- Section 2A1.1-2: Definitions

D. Statement of Authority

This subchapter is based on the law cited below.

- United States Code: 5 U.S.C. 8462

Part 2B2 Computation

Section 2B2.1-1 Computation of COLA'S

A. Eligibility

FERS COLA's do not apply to annuitants who are under age 62 as of December 1, except:

1. Disability annuitants, including military reserve technicians who are medically disqualified for military service or the rank required to hold their positions. However, disability annuitants who are receiving 60 percent of their average salary do not receive COLA's.

2. Military reserve technicians whose separation from technician service resulted from loss of military membership or rank on account of disability after attaining age 50 and completing 25 years of service.

3. Employees who retired under the special provisions for law enforcement officers, firefighters, or air traffic controllers.

4. Spouse, former spouse, and insurable interest survivor annuitants.

NOTE 1: Under FERS, children's annuities are increased under CSRS provisions rather than FERS provisions.

NOTE 2: Under CSRS rules, retirees may receive a COLA at any age.

Cost-of-Living Adjustments **FERS**
Chapter 2

Section 2B2.1-1 Computation of COLA'S (Cont.)

B. COLA Rate As under CSRS, the amount of a COLA is determined by the percent change in the base quarter price index from the previous year to the year in which the COLA is to become effective adjusted to the nearest 1/10 of 1 percent.

Generally, FERS COLA's are 1 percent less than the increase in the CPI as determined under the law. However, if the CPI increase is between 2 and 3 percent the FERS COLA is 2 percent. If the actual increase is 2 percent or less, the FERS COLA matches the CPI increase.

The following table summarizes the above information.

If the Increase in CPI Is	Then the Annual FERS COLA Is
Up to 2.0%	Same as CPI
2.0% to 3.0%	2.0%
Above 3.0%	CPI increase minus 1.0%

EXAMPLE:

Year	Base Quarter Price Index
1988	117.8
1987	113.3
Difference	4.5

$$\frac{4.5}{113.3} \times 100 = 3.97\% \text{ (CPI increase)}$$

$$3.97\% - 1.00\% = 2.97\%$$

COLA Rate = 3.0% (adjusted to the nearest 1/10 of 1%) effective December 1, 1988

Section 2B2.1-1 Computation of COLA'S (Cont.)

C. COLA Increase	The CSRS rules in section 2A2.1-1 on how to determine the COLA increase generally apply under FERS; however, the gross monthly annuity used in the FERS COLA computation is defined a little differently. The FERS gross monthly annuity is the annuity payable after the following adjustments (when applicable) have been made: • Reduction for survivor benefits; • Reduction for alternative annuity; • Reduction for early retirement under MRA + 10 and early deferred provisions. NOTE 1: The CSRS reduction for pre-October 1, 1982, deposit service does not apply to FERS annuities that do not have a CSRS component. NOTE 2: See section 2B6.1-1, paragraph A for the rules covering disability retirees.
D. Disability Annuitants	When a disability annuity increases because of a COLA, the reduction (if any) for the Social Security benefit also increases. (See Chapter 60, Disability Retirement.)

Part 2B3 Proration

Section 2B3.1-1 Proration of First COLA

A. General Rule

The rules in section 2A3.1-1 on proration of the first COLA for CSRS apply under FERS.

For FERS annuitants who are not eligible to receive a COLA during their first year (or more) on the annuity roll, the initial COLA they receive (after becoming eligible) is the full COLA without proration. The annuitants who fall in this category are:

- Annuitants under age 62 whose annuity commences at least 1 year prior to reaching age 62;

- Disability annuitants whose annuity benefits are based on 60 percent of average pay.

EXAMPLE 1: Bill retired at age 59. He will become 62 in July 1990. In January 1991, he will receive an unprorated COLA.

EXAMPLE 2: Jane is a disability retiree. From July 1, 1988, to June 30, 1989, she received 60 percent of her high-3. On July 1, 1989 she began receiving 40 percent of her high-3. In January 1990, she will receive an unprorated COLA.

Part 2B4 Transfer Employees With a CSRS Component

Section 2B4.1-1 Transfer Employees With a CSRS Component

A. Transfer Employees With a CSRS Component

Certain FERS annuitants are entitled to a CSRS annuity computation for a portion of their annuity. The CSRS portion of the annuity is subject to CSRS COLA rules, rather than FERS COLA rules.

CSRS COLA rules do not require the annuitant to be age 62. Therefore, the CSRS portion of the annuity may increase even though no FERS increase is payable.

Cost-of-Living Adjustments
Chapter 2

FERS 15

Part 2B5 Survivor Annuities and Death Benefit

Section 2B5.1-1 Survivor Annuities

A. Spouse, Former Spouse, Insurable Interest	1. An annuity payable to a FERS retiree's survivor normally commences on the day after death.
	2. FERS survivor annuities are increased by COLA's after they commence even though the survivor annuitant is not yet age 62. The proration rules in Part 2B2 apply to the first COLA paid to the survivor of a retiree who dies before having been retired for a year or to the survivor of an employee who died in service.
	EXAMPLE 1: Retiree is age 59 when he retires in June 1989. He dies at age 61 in June 1991. The retiree had not received a COLA because he had not reached age 62. In December 1991, the survivor annuity receives a full COLA because the retiree's annuity had begun more than a year earlier.
	EXAMPLE 2: Same as Example 1 except that retiree dies in November 1989. In December 1989, the survivor annuity (which commenced in November) receives a prorated COLA based on the fact that the deceased retiree's annuity commenced in June. (Half of the regular COLA would be payable because 6 months had passed.)
	3. When a retiree dies, the potential survivor benefit calculated at retirement is increased by the total percent that the retiree's annuity had increased since retirement. If the retiree had received no COLA increases because he or she was under age 62, there is no increase in the survivor benefit. On the effective date of the next COLA, the survivor annuity increase is determined based on the length of time that has passed since the annuity was first payable to the deceased retiree. If at least one year has passed since the deceased retiree's annuity commenced, the survivor annuity is increased by a full COLA. If less than one year has passed, the COLA is prorated based on the retiree's annuity commencing date.
	4. FERS survivor annuities do not have CSRS components. The entire survivor annuity is subject to FERS COLA rules, even if it is based on a basic employee annuity that includes a CSRS component.
B. Children	Cost-of-living adjustments for children's annuities under FERS are determined under CSRS rules. (See section 2A4.1-1).

Section 2B5.1-2 Death Benefit

CSRS and FERS Handbook — April 1998

A. Lump-Sum Death Benefit	The FERS basic employee death benefit (see Chapter 70, Spouse Benefits - Death of an Employee) is an amount equal to 50 percent of the employee's final pay (or average pay, if higher) plus $15,000 adjusted for COLA's under CSRS rules. See subchapter 2C for lump-sum benefit amounts for each COLA increase.

Part 2B6 Miscellaneous

Section 2B6.1-1 Miscellaneous COLA Provisions

A. Disability Annuitants

1. COLA's are not payable on disability annuities during the annuitant's first year on the annuity roll if the annuity rate is based on 60 percent of his or her average salary. If an annuitant is removed from the roll for recovery or restoration to earning capacity, he or she is restored at the 60 percent rate for a year and not eligible for COLA's for that year.

2. COLA's are payable during the first year if:

   - The annuitant's rate is based on an earned benefit; or

   - The annuity is recomputed because the annuitant has reached age 62.

   NOTE: The Social Security offset also does not increase by COLA's during the first year.

3. After the first year, both the disability annuity and the Social Security offset increase under the FERS COLA rules.

4. Even though the disability annuity may include 5 or more years of creditable CSRS service, the disability annuity is increased totally under FERS COLA rules, unless:

   - The annuitant's rate is based on an earned benefit that includes a CSRS component; or

   - The annuity is recomputed because the annuitant has reached age 62 and includes a CSRS component.

B. Reemployed Annuitants

The CSRS rule in section 2A5.1-1 for reemployed annuitants applies under FERS.

BLANK PAGE

CSRS Cost-of-Living Adjustments
Chapter 2

Subchapter 2C Job Aids

Section 2C1.1-1 Copies of Job Aids

TABLE OF CSRS COLA's FOR FEDERAL RETIREES

	Effective Date	Year	Amount of Increase
>	December 1	1997	2.1%
	December 1	1996	2.9%
	December 1	1995**	2.6%
	December 1	1994**	2.8%
	December 1	1993**	2.6% <
	December 1	1992	3.0%
	December 1	1991	3.7%
	December 1	1990	5.4%
	December 1	1989	4.7%
	December 1	1988	4.0%
	December 1	1987	4.2%
	December 1	1986	1.3%
	December 1	1985	No Increase
	December 1	1984	3.5%
	April 1	1983	3.9%*
	March 1	1982	8.7%
	March 1	1981	4.4%
	September 1	1980	7.7%
	March 1	1980	6.0%
	September 1	1979	6.9%
	March 1	1979	3.9%
	September 1	1978	4.9%
	March 1	1978	2.4%
	September 1	1977	4.3%
	March 1	1977	4.8%
	March 1	1976	5.4%
	August 1	1975	5.1%
	January 1	1975	7.3%
	July 1	1974	6.3%
	January 1	1974	5.5%
	July 1	1973	6.1%
	July 1	1972	4.8%
	June 1	1971	4.5%
	August 1	1970	5.6%
	November 1	1969	5.0%
	March 1	1969	3.9%
	May 1	1968	3.9%
	January 1	1967	3.9%

*3.3% for non-disabled employee annuitants under age 62

** Payment of these COLAS was delayed until March 1 of the following year.

Section 2C1.1-1 Copies of Job Aids (Cont.)

TABLE OF FERS COLA'S FOR FEDERAL RETIREES

	Effective Date	Year	Amount of Increase	
>	December 1	1997	2.0%	
	December 1	1996	2.0%	
	December 1	1995*	2.0%	
	December 1	1994*	2.0%	
	December 1	1993*	2.0%	<
	December 1	1992	2.0%	
	December 1	1991	2.7%	
	December 1	1990	4.4%	
	December 1	1989	3.7%	
	December 1	1988	3.0%	
	December 1	1987	3.2%	

* Payment of these COLAs was delayed until March 1 of the following year

Section 2C1.1-1 Copies of Job Aids (Cont.)

TABLE OF COLA ADJUSTMENTS TO $15,000 PORTION OF
FERS BASIC EMPLOYEE DEATH BENEFIT

The law provides that the FERS Basic Employee Death Benefit is an amount equal to 50 percent of the employee's final annual pay (or average pay, if higher), plus $15,000, adjusted for COLA's under CSRS rules.

	Effective Date	**Year**	**CSRS COLA**	**Basic Benefit Amount**
>	December 1	1997	2.1%	$21,783.34
	December 1	1996	2.9%	$21,335.30
	December 1	1995*	2.6%	$20,734.01
	December 1	1994*	2.8%	$20,208.59
	December 1	1993*	2.6	$19,658.16 <
	December 1	1992	3.0	$19,160.00
	December 1	1991	3.7	$18,601.94
	December 1	1990	5.4%	$17,938.23
	December 1	1989	4.7%	$17,019.19
	December 1	1988	4.0%	$16,255.20
	December 1	1987	4.2%	$15,630.00
	January 1	1987	N/A	$15,000.00

NOTE 1: Recipients of this death benefit are entitled to a COLA if the employee died on or after the effective date of that COLA.

NOTE 2: The COLA effective December 1, 1997 for retirees is effective for death benefit recipients in any case in which the employee dies on or after December 1, 1996, and before December 1, 1997.

*Payment of these COLAs was delayed until March 1 of the following year.

CSRS / FERS
Reconsideration and Appeal
Chapter 3

Table of Contents

Subchapter 3A CSRS and FERS

Part 3A1 General Information

Section 3A1 Overview 1
A. Introduction 1
B. Topics Covered 1
C. Organization of Subchapter 1
D. Statement of Authority 1

Part 3A2 Reconsideration

Section 3A2.1-1 Request for Reconsideration 2
A. General Rule 2
B. Exception: Final Initial Decisions 2
C. Content of Reconsideration Request 2
D. Time Limit on Filing Reconsideration Request 2
E. Final Reconsideration Decisions 2

Section 3A2.1-2 Competing Claimants 3
A. Competing Claimants 3
B. Notification Requirement 3
C. Final Reconsideration Decisions Involving Competing Claimants 3

Part 3A3 Appeal

Section 3A3.1-1 Appeal to the Merit Systems Protection Board (MSPB) 4
A. General Rule 4
B. The MSPB 4

CSRS Reconsideration and Appeal FERS
Chapter 3

Subchapter 3A CSRS and FERS
Part 3A1 General Information

Section 3A1.1-1 Overview

A. Introduction

This chapter explains the rules that apply to requests for reconsideration and/or appeals of OPM decisions.

B. Topics Covered

This chapter covers the procedures an individual must follow to request reconsideration of an initial OPM decision or to appeal a final OPM decision.

NOTE 1: See Chapter 11, Elections of FERS Coverage, for the procedures an agency must follow in making initial decisions about certain elections to transfer to FERS.

NOTE 2: See Chapter 46, Special Retirement Provisions for Law Enforcement Officers, Firefighters, Air Traffic Controllers, and National Guard Technicians, for the procedures an agency must follow in making coverage determinations for law enforcement officers and firefighters.

C. Organization of Subchapter

This subchapter has three parts.

Part	Name of Part	Page
3A1	General Information	1
3A2	Reconsideration	2
3A3	Appeal	4

D. Statement of Authority

This chapter and its contents are based on the laws and regulations cited below.

- United States Code: 5 U.S.C. 8347(d) and 5 U.S.C. 8461(e)(1)

- Code of Federal Regulations: 5 CFR 831.109-110 and 5 CFR 841.305-309

Part 3A2 Reconsideration

Section 3A2.1-1 Request for Reconsideration

A.	**General Rule**	Generally, any individual whose rights or interests under CSRS or FERS are affected by a decision of OPM may request OPM to review its initial decision.
		A decision is considered an initial decision when rendered by OPM in writing and stating the right of reconsideration.
B.	**Exception: Final Initial Decisions**	When circumstances warrant, OPM's initial decision will be issued as a final decision. Such decisions provide a direct appeal right to the Merit Systems Protection Board (MSPB). (See part 3A3.)
C.	**Content of Reconsideration Request**	A request for reconsideration must be in writing, must include the individual's name, address, date of birth, and claim number (if applicable), and must state the basis for the request.
D.	**Time Limit on Filing Reconsideration Request**	A request for reconsideration must be received by OPM within 30 calendar days from the date of the initial decision.
		OPM may extend the time limit for filing when the individual shows that he or she:
		• Was not notified of the time limit and was not otherwise aware of it; or
		• Was prevented by circumstances beyond his or her control from making the request within the time limit.
E.	**Final Reconsideration Decisions**	OPM will issue a final reconsideration decision in writing. The decision will set forth the findings and conclusions of the reconsideration in full and contain notice of the right to appeal. (See part 3A3.)
		Copies of the final reconsideration decision will be sent to the individual, to any competing claimants, and where applicable, to the agency.

Section 3A2.1-2 Competing Claimants

A. Competing Claimants

Competing claimants are applicants for survivor benefits based on the service of a deceased employee, separated employee, or retiree when:

1. An annuity or lump-sum benefit is payable based on the service of the deceased employee, separated employee, or retiree;

2. Two or more claimants have applied for an annuity or lump-sum benefit based on the service of the deceased employee, separated employee, or retiree; and

3. An OPM decision in favor of one claimant will adversely affect another claimant(s).

B. Notification Requirement

When a competing claimant files a request for reconsideration, OPM notifies the other competing claimants of the request and gives them an opportunity to submit written substantiation of their claim.

C. Final Reconsideration Decisions Involving Competing Claimants

In cases involving competing claimants, OPM will issue a final reconsideration decision in writing. The decision will set forth the findings and conclusions of the reconsideration in full and contain notice of the right of appeal. (See part 3A3.)

Copies of the final reconsideration decision will be sent to all competing claimants.

Part 3A3 Appeal

Section 3A3.1-1 Appeal to the Merit Systems Protection Board (MSPB)

A. General Rule An individual whose rights or interests under CSRS or FERS are affected by a final decision of OPM may request MSPB to review the decision in accordance with procedures prescribed by the Board.

NOTE: When OPM issues a final decision appealable to MSPB, the decision includes instructions on how to file an appeal.

EXCEPTION: An OPM determination that payment of annuity is barred by subchapter II of chapter 83 of title 5, U.S. Code (concerning persons convicted of offenses involving national security violations) is not appealable to MSPB.

NOTE: OPM decisions concerning entitlements under the Federal Employees Health Benefits and Federal Employees Group Life Insurance programs are not appealable to MSPB.

B. The MSPB The MSPB is an independent Government agency created to ensure that all Federal agencies follow Federal merit systems practices, and to allow employees to appeal certain personnel actions by Federal agencies.

NOTE: The regulations that describe the organization and procedures of the MSPB are found in 5 CFR Part 1200 et seq.

CSRS   Debt Collection   FERS
Chapter 4

Table of Contents

Part 4A1 General Information

Section 4A1.1-1 Overview 1
- A. Introduction 1
- B. Topics Covered 1
- C. Organization of Chapter 1
- D. Statement of Authority 1

Section 4A1.1-2 Definitions 2
- A. Administrative Offset 2
- B. Agency 2
- C. Creditor Agency 2
- D. Debt Claim 2
- E. Debtor 2
- F. FCCS 2
- G. Fraud Claim 2
- H. Net Annuity 2
- I. Offset 3
- J. Paying Agency 3
- K. Waiver 3

Part 4A2 Agency Requests to OPM for Recovery of a Debt From the Retirement Fund

Subpart 4A2.1 General

Section 4A2.1-1 General 4
- A. Purpose 4
- B. Limitation on Collection 4
- C. Limitations on OPM Review 4
- D. Conditions for Requesting an Offset 5
- E. Standard Form (SF) 2805 5

Subpart 4A2.2 Creditor Agency Procedures for Non-Fraud Claims

Section 4A2.2-1 Where to Submit the Debt Claim, Judgment, or Notice of Debt 6
- A. Creditor Agencies that Are Not Debtor's Paying Agency 6
- B. Creditor Agencies that Are Debtor's Paying Agency 6

**Section 4A2.2-2 Procedures for Submitting a Debt Claim, Judgment, or Notice of
Debt to OPM** 7
A. Debt Claims for Which the Agency Has a Court Judgment 7
B. Debt Claims Previously Processed Under
5 U.S.C. 5514 7
C. Debt Claims Not Being Processed as a Judgment Offset, a Continuation of a
Previously Established Salary Offset, or a Claim Excepted
by Paragraph D 7
D. Debt Claims Excepted from Procedures Described in Paragraph C 8
E. General Certification Requirements for Claims Against Retirement Benefits 8
F. Notice of Debt in Lieu of SF 2805 9

Section 4A2.2-3 Procedures for Recovering Health Benefits Premiums 11
A. General 11

Section 4A2.2-4 Time Limits for Sending Records and Debt Claims to OPM 12
A. Time Limits for Submitting Debt Claims 12
B. Time Limit for Submitting Retirement Records to OPM 12

Subpart 4A2.3 OPM Processing for Non-Fraud Claims

Section 4A2.3-1 Refunds--Incomplete Debt Claims 13
A. General 13
B. Time Limits for Filing Completed Debt Claim 13
C. OPM Action on Refund Application 13

Section 4A2.3-2 Refunds--Complete Debt Claims 14
A. If OPM Receives Application from Debtor Prior to or at Same Time as Agency's
Claim 14
B. If OPM Has Not Received Application from Debtor When the Agency's Debt
Claim is Received 14
C. Future Recovery 14

Section 4A2.3-3 Annuities--Incomplete Debt Claims 16
A. General 16

Section 4A2.3-4 Annuities--Complete Debt Claims 17
A. General 17
B. Claims Held for Future Recovery 17

Subpart 4A2.4 Installment Withholdings

Section 4A2.4-1 Installment Withholdings 19
- A. General 19
- B. Rule 19
- C. Limitation on Installment Withholdings 19

Subpart 4A2.5 Special Processing for Fraud Claims

Section 4A2.5-1 Special Processing for Fraud Claims 20
- A. General 20
- B. Agency Processing 20
- C. Department of Justice Processing 20
- D. Agency Processing of a Claim Returned by the Department of Justice .. 21
- E. OPM Processing Against Refunds 21
- F. OPM Processing Against Annuities 22
- G. OPM Collection and Payment of the Debt 22

CSRS Debt Collection Chapter 4 FERS

Part 4A1 General Information

Section 4A1.1-1 Overview

A. Introduction

This chapter describes the procedures to be followed by a Federal agency when it requests the Office of Personnel Management (OPM) to recover a debt owed to the United States by administrative or judgment offset against money due and payable from the debtor from the Civil Service Retirement and Disability Fund (the Fund). It also describes the procedures that OPM must follow to make these administrative offsets.

B. Topics Covered

This chapter covers:

- Creditor agency procedures when requesting OPM to recover non-fraud debt claims;

- OPM processing of incomplete and complete debt claims involving refunds and annuities; and

- Special processing procedures for fraud claims.

C. Organization of Chapter

This chapter has two parts.

Part	Name of Part	Page
4A1	General Information	1
4A2	Agency Requests to OPM for Recovery of a Debt From the Retirement Fund	4

D. Statement of Authority

This chapter and its contents are based on the laws and regulations cited below.

- United States Code: 31 U.S.C. 3716, 5 U.S.C. 5514, 5 U.S.C. 8347, 5 U.S.C. 8461 and Section 124 of P.L. 97-276, 96 Stat. 1195-1196

- Code of Federal Regulations: 5 CFR Part 831, Subparts M and R; 5 CFR Part 845

Section 4A1.1-2 Definitions

A. Administrative Offset

"Administrative offset" means withholding money payable from the Fund to satisfy a debt to the United States as authorized under the provisions of 31 U.S.C. 3716.

B. Agency

"Agency" means:

1. An Executive agency as defined in 5 U.S.C. 105, including the U.S. Postal Service and the U.S. Postal Rate Commission;

2. A military department, as defined in 5 U.S.C. 102;

3. An agency or court in the judicial branch, including a court as defined in the 28 U.S.C. 610, the District Court for the Northern Mariana Islands, and the Judicial Panel on Multidistrict Litigation;

4. An agency of the legislative branch, including the U.S. Senate and the U.S. House of Representatives; and

5. Other independent establishments that are entities of the Federal government.

C. Creditor Agency

"Creditor agency" means the agency to which the debt is owed.

D. Debt Claim

"Debt claim" means an agency request for recovery of debt in a form approved by OPM.

E. Debtor

"Debtor" means a person who owes a debt, including an employee, former employee, Member, former member, or the survivor of one of these individuals.

F. FCCS

"FCCS" means the Federal Claims Collection Standards (Chapter II of Title 4, Code of Federal Regulations).

G. Fraud Claim

"Fraud claim" means any debt designated by the Attorney General or designee as involving an indication of fraud, the presentation of a false claim, or misrepresentation on the part of any other party having an interest in the claim.

H. Net Annuity

"Net annuity" means annuity after excluding amounts required by law to be deducted. For example, Federal income tax is excluded up to the maximum amount that the individual is entitled to for all dependents.

Section 4A1.1-2 Definitions (Cont.)

H.	**Net Annuity (Cont.)**	Other examples of exclusions are group health insurance premiums, including amounts deducted for Medicare, and group life insurance premiums.
I.	**Offset**	"Offset" means to withhold the amount of a debt, or a portion of that amount, from one or more payments due the debtor. Offset also means the amount withheld in this manner.
J.	**Paying Agency**	"Paying agency" means the agency that employs the debtor and/or authorizes the disbursement of his or her current pay or benefits.
K.	**Waiver**	"Waiver" is a decision by OPM not to recover a debt owed to the retirement fund as authorized by 5 U.S.C. 8345(b) and 5 CFR 831.1401 et seq. or 5 U.S.C. 8470 and 5 CFR 845.301 et seq.

Debt Collection
Chapter 4

Part 4A2 Agency Requests to OPM for Recovery of a Debt From the Retirement Fund
Subpart 4A2.1 General

Section 4A2.1-1 General

A. Purpose

This part describes the procedures to be followed by a Federal agency when it requests OPM to recover a debt owed to the United States by administrative or judgment offset against money due and payable to the debtor from the Fund.

B. Limitation on Collection

Generally, debts may be collected from retirement benefits only to the extent expressly authorized by Federal statutes. As an agency of the Federal Government, OPM will collect claims such as:

1. Debts due other Federal agencies, as authorized by 31 U.S.C. 3716;

2. Debts, penalties, and interest due because of a court judgment obtained by the Department of Justice or its designee, as authorized by Public Law 97-276, 96 Stat. 1195-1196; and

3. Alimony or child support, as authorized by 42 U.S.C. 659. (See discussion in Chapter 5.)

NOTE: Unliquidated unearned (advanced) annual and sick leave does not constitute a valid indebtedness when the employee is separated by death or retirement for disability, or when the employee is unable to return to duty because of disability evidenced by an acceptable medical certificate. Requests for collection of such debts should not be sent to OPM.

C. Limitations on OPM Review

OPM reviews an agency's certification of due process required by 4 CFR 102.4(b). However, all due process procedures and protests of creditor agency collection actions **must** be handled by the creditor agency. If debtors have a dispute with the creditor agency concerning the amount or validity of the debt or the terms of the collection schedule, they must resolve the dispute directly with the agency. If the creditor agency's request for offset meets all requirements, OPM makes the offset even though the debtor is protesting the collection. The creditor agency should make it clear to the debtor that OPM is only making the collection at the agency's request and give the debtor an agency contact and address for any questions about the debt or the installment schedule.

Section 4A2.1-1 General (Cont.)

C. Limitations on OPM Review (Cont.)

OPM does not have the authority to review:

- The adequacy of the due process procedures that have been provided to a debtor;

- The merits of a creditor agency's decision with regard to reconsideration, compromise, or waiver, or

- The creditor agency's decision that a hearing was not required in any particular proceeding.

OPM merely implements the collection decisions made by the creditor agency. OPM's acceptance of an agency's certification, if it is valid on its face, does not provide the debtor with a second opportunity for review of the merits of the agency's claim.

D. Conditions for Requesting an Offset

An agency may request that money payable from the Fund be offset to recover any valid debt due the United States when all of the following conditions are met:

1. The debtor failed to pay all of the debt on demand, or the creditor agency has collected as much as possible from payments due the debtor from the paying agency; and

2. The creditor agency sends a debt claim to OPM (see section 4A2.2-2, paragraphs A through D, as appropriate) after doing one of the following:

   - Obtaining a court judgment for the amount of the debt and following the procedures prescribed by the U.S. Department of Justice for judgment offsets;

   - Following the procedures required by 31 U.S.C. 3716 and 4 CFR 102.4; or

   - Following the procedures agreed upon by the creditor agency and OPM, if the creditor agency is pursuing a debt described in section 4A2.2-2, paragraph D.

E. Standard Form (SF) 2805

Unless the agency or the type of claim has been specifically excepted by OPM, an agency's debt claim must be filed on SF 2805, Request for Recovery of a Debt Due the United States.

Subpart 4A2.2 Creditor Agency Procedures for Non-Fraud Claims

Section 4A2.2-1 Where to Submit the Debt Claim, Judgment, or Notice of Debt

A. Creditor Agencies that Are Not Debtor's Paying Agency	If the creditor agency knows that the debtor is employed by the Federal Government, it should send the debt claim to the debtor's paying agency for collection by salary offset as provided under 5 U.S.C. 5514. If some of the debt is unpaid after the debtor separates from the paying agency, the creditor agency may send the debt claim to OPM for collection under 31 U.S.C. 3716, as described in section 4A2.2-2 below.
B. Creditor Agencies that Are Debtor's Paying Agency	Ordinarily, debts owed to the debtor's paying agency should be offset under the authority of 31 U.S.C. 3716 from any final payments (salary, accrued annual leave, etc.) due the debtor. If a balance is due after offsetting the final payments or the debt is discovered after the debtor has been paid, the paying agency may send a debt claim to OPM as described in section 4A2.2-2 below.

Section 4A2.2-2 Procedures for Submitting a Debt Claim, Judgment, or Notice of Debt to OPM

A. Debt Claims for Which the Agency Has a Court Judgment	If the creditor agency has a court judgment against the debtor specifying the amount of the debt to be recovered, the agency or the Department of Justice should send an SF 2805 and two certified copies of the judgment to OPM for recovery.	
B. Debt Claims Previously Processed Under 5 U.S.C. 5514	If the creditor agency has been collecting the debt under 5 U.S.C. 5514, it must:	
	1.	Notify the debtor that the claim is being sent to OPM to **complete** collection of the debt by offsetting benefits payable from the Fund; and
	2.	Send SF 2805 to OPM with two copies of the paying agency's certification of the amount collected and one copy of the notice to the debtor explaining that the claim was sent to OPM to complete the collection.
C. Debt Claims Not Being Processed as a Judgment Offset, a Continuation of a Previously Established Salary Offset, or a Claim Excepted by Paragraph D	1.	If the debt claim is not a judgment offset, a continuation of a collection previously established as a salary offset, or a claim excepted by paragraph D (below), the creditor agency must:
		• Issue a written notice to the debtor explaining the nature and amount of the debt, the agency's intention to collect by administrative offset from the debtor's retirement benefits, the opportunity to inspect and copy agency records pertaining to the debt, the opportunity to obtain a review within the creditor agency of the determination of indebtedness, and the opportunity to enter into a written agreement with the creditor agency to repay the debt (see 4 CFR 102.4); and
		• Complete SF 2805, Request for Recovery of a Debt Due the United States.
	2.	If the debtor does not respond to the creditor agency's notice within the allotted time and there is no reason to believe that he or she did not receive the notice, the creditor agency may submit SF 2805 to OPM after certifying that notice was issued and the debtor failed to reply.

Section 4A2.2-2 Procedures for Submitting a Debt Claim, Judgment, or Notice of Debt to OPM (Cont.)

C. Debt Claims Not Being Processed as a Judgment Offset, a Continuation of a Previously Established Salary Offset, or a Claim Excepted by Paragraph D (Cont.)

3. If the debtor responds to the notice by requesting a review or hearing, if one is available, the review or hearing must be completed before the creditor agency submits SF 2805. The creditor agency must show on the SF 2805, the date the review or hearing ended in a decision for the agency.

4. If the debtor receives the notice and responds by consenting to the collection, the creditor agency must send a copy of the debtor's consent along with the SF 2805.

D. Debt Claims Excepted from Procedures Described in Paragraph C

Certain creditor agencies follow specific procedures approved by OPM, rather than those described in paragraph C, for the collection of:

1. Debts due because of the individual's failure to pay health benefits premiums while he or she was in nonpay status or while his or her salary was not sufficient to cover the cost of premiums (see section 4A2.2-3 below);

2. Unpaid Federal taxes to be collected by Internal Revenue Service levy;

3. Premiums due because of the annuitant's election of Medicare Part B coverage (retroactive collection is limited to 6 months of premiums); or

4. Overpayments that occur as a result of a delay in terminating the retiree's military retired pay when he or she elects in writing to have it withheld from his or her annuity.

E. General Certification Requirements for Claims Against Retirement Benefits

Creditor agencies submitting claims must certify:

1. That the debt is owed to the United States;

2. The amount and reason for the debt and whether additional interest accrues;

3. The date the Government's right to collect the debt first accrued;

Section 4A2.2-2 Procedures for Submitting a Debt Claim, Judgment, or Notice of Debt to OPM (Cont.)

E. General Certification

4. That the agency has complied with the applicable statutes, regulations, and OPM procedures;

Requirements for Claims Against Retirement Benefits (Cont.)

5. A specific dollar amount or specific percentage of net annuity for collections that must be completed in installments;

6. If the debtor consents to the collection from the Fund or acknowledges the debt in writing, a copy of the debtor's written consent or acknowledgement. If there is no written consent or acknowledgement, the creditor agency must certify the date of the initial demand letter and the actions taken to comply with the due process requirements of 4 CFR 102.3 --

   - Show the date of the **initial notice** of the collection, **and** the date(s) of any additional applicable actions, such as (1) the date the debtor's failure to respond to the initial notice allowed the creditor agency to assume consent to the collection, **or** (2) if the debtor did respond, the date the debtor requested review of the debt, **and** the date the review or hearing--if applicable--was held, **and** the date the review or hearing was decided in favor of the creditor agency; and

7. That if a competent administrative or judicial authority issues an order directing OPM to pay a debtor an amount previously paid to the agency (regardless of the reasons behind the order), the agency will reimburse OPM or pay the debtor directly within 15 days of the date of the order.

   NOTE: If an agency does not make the required reimbursement when requested, OPM may decline to collect other claims for that agency.

F. Notice of Debt in Lieu of SF 2805

When a creditor agency cannot send an SF 2805, it should notify OPM of the existence of the debt so a refund will not be paid before the claim arrives. OPM **will not** withhold payment of monthly annuity or retroactive accrued annuity unless the agency and the debtor have concluded specific negotiations concerning the payment of such benefits and OPM is given specific direction concerning the terms of such an agreement. Otherwise, collections will only be made against prospective annuity payments.

CSRS Debt Collection Chapter 4 FERS

Section 4A2.2-2 Procedures for Submitting a Debt Claim, Judgment, or Notice of Debt to OPM (Cont.)

F. Notice of Debt in Lieu of SF 2805 (Cont.)

1. The notice to OPM must include a statement that the debt is owed to the United States, the date the debt first accrued, and the basis for and amount of the debt, if known. If the amount of the debt is not known, the agency must establish the amount and notify OPM in writing as soon as possible after submitting the notice.

2. The creditor agency may notify OPM by making a notation in column 8 (Remarks) under the "Fiscal Record" portion of the Individual Retirement Record (SF 2806 or SF 3100), if the SF 2806/SF 3100 is in its possession, or if not, by submitting a separate document identifying the debtor by name, giving his or her date of birth, Social Security number, and date of separation, if known.

Section 4A2.2-3 Procedures for Recovering Health Benefits Premiums

A. General

Agencies may recover past-due health benefits premiums from separated employees by requesting OPM to withhold the premium amount from any payments due the former employee, including refunds due employees who have separated and annuities due employees who have retired.

The agency must submit OPM Form 1522 to request an offset for past-due health benefits premiums from any amounts to be paid to a separated employee from the retirement system. (SF 2805 will not be accepted.) In addition, the SF 2806 or SF 3100 should be noted when forwarded to OPM to show that the separating employee is indebted.

Section 4A2.2-4 Time Limits for Sending Records and Debt Claims to OPM

A. Time Limits for Submitting Debt Claims

1. Unless there is an application for a refund pending, there is no specific time for submitting a debt claim or notice of debt to OPM. Generally, however, agencies must file a debt claim before the statute of limitations expires (4 CFR 102.4(c)) or before a refund is paid.

2. Time limits are imposed when the debtor is eligible for a refund and OPM receives his or her application requesting payment (see section 4A2.3-1). Creditor agencies must file SF 2805 or other claim within 120 days -- 180 days if the agency requests an extension of time before the refund is paid -- of the date OPM requests a complete debt claim.

B. Time Limit for Submitting Retirement Records to OPM

1. Generally, a paying agency must send an individual's SF 2806 or SF 3100 to OPM no later than 30 days after the separation, termination, or entrance on duty in a position in which the employee is not covered by CSRS or FERS.

2. If the agency's claim is based on circumstances that indicate fraud (such as presentation of a false claim or misrepresentation by the debtor or some other party having an interest in the claim) and require the claim to be submitted to the Department of Justice, the agency may have an additional 30 days -- a total of 60 days -- to submit the record to OPM. In the latter case, the agency must notify OPM that the case is under consideration by the Department of Justice.

Subpart 4A2.3 OPM Processing for Non-Fraud Claims

Section 4A2.3-1 Refunds--Incomplete Debt Claims

A. General

If a creditor agency sends OPM a notice of debt or an incomplete debt claim against a refund OPM is processing for payment, OPM will withhold the amount of the debt but will not make any payment to the creditor agency. OPM will notify the creditor agency that the procedures described in this part and 4 CFR 102.4 must be completed and a properly completed SF 2805 submitted to OPM by a specified date.

B. Time Limits for Filing Completed Debt Claim

Generally, a debt claim must be completed and returned to OPM within 120 days of the date of OPM's notice to the creditor agency. However, upon request, OPM will grant the creditor agency one extension of up to 60 days if the request for extension is received before the lump-sum payment has been made. The extension will commence on the day after the 120-day period expires so that the total time OPM holds payment of the refund will not exceed 180 days.

C. OPM Action on Refund Application

During the period allotted a creditor agency for sending OPM an SF 2806 or SF 3100, OPM will do the following:

1. If the amount of the debt is known, OPM will notify the debtor of the claim against his or her lump-sum credit, withhold the amount of the debt, and pay the balance to the debtor, if any.

2. If the amount of the debt is not known, OPM will not pay the debtor until the creditor agency certifies the amount of the debt, submits an SF 2805, or the time limit for submission of the claim expires, whichever comes first.

Section 4A2.3-2 Refunds--Complete Debt Claims

A. If OPM Receives Application from Debtor Prior to or at Same Time as Agency's Claim

1. If a refund has been paid, OPM will notify the creditor agency there are no funds available for offset. Except in the case of debts due because of the employee's failure to pay health benefits premiums while he or she is in nonpay status or while his or her salary was not sufficient to cover the cost of premiums, creditor agencies should refer to the instructions in the FCCS for other measures to recover the outstanding debt; however, OPM will retain the SF 2805 on file in the event the debtor is once again employed in a position subject to retirement deductions.

2. If a refund is payable, and the creditor agency submits a claim in accordance with section 4A2.2-2, paragraphs A through D, the debt will be collected from the refund and any balance paid to the debtor. OPM will send the debtor a copy of the agency's claim, judgment, his or her written consent, or other document, and notify him or her that the creditor agency was paid.

B. If OPM Has Not Received Application from Debtor When the Agency's Debt Claim is Received

If a debtor has not filed application for a refund, OPM will file the claim for future recovery. OPM will make the collection whenever an application is received, provided the creditor agency initiated the administrative offset before the statute of limitations expired. [See 4 CFR 102.3(b)(3) and 102.4(c).] OPM will notify the creditor agency that it has filed the claim for future recovery because we do not have an application from the debtor. The agency may take other actions to recover the debt in the interim.

NOTE: If the other recovery action is successful, the creditor agency must notify OPM so it can void the debt claim.

C. Future Recovery

1. If OPM receives an application for a refund within 1 year of the date the agency's claim was received and the creditor agency does not indicate that interest is accruing on the debt, the debt will be processed as stated in paragraph A2 above.

2. If OPM receives an application for a refund within 1 year of the date the agency's debt claim was received and the creditor agency indicates that interest accrues on the debt, when necessary, OPM will contact the creditor agency to confirm that the debt is outstanding and request submission in writing, of the total additional accrued interest. **OPM will not make interest computations for creditor agencies.**

CSRS   Debt Collection   FERS
Chapter 4

Section 4A2.3-2 Refunds--Complete Debt Claims (Cont.)

C. **Future Recovery (Cont.)**

3. When OPM receives an application for a refund more than 1 year after the creditor agency's debt claim was received, whether interest accrues or not, OPM will contact the creditor agency to see if the debt is still outstanding and, when necessary, request an update of the interest charges.

   If the debt is still due, the creditor agency should give the debtor an opportunity to offer a satisfactory repayment plan instead of the offset if the debtor establishes that his or her changed financial circumstances, if any, would make the offset unjust. (See 4 CFR 102.4(c).)

   If the agency decides to pursue the offset, it must submit to OPM the requested information and any new instructions within 60 days of the date of OPM's request or the claim may be voided and the balance paid to the individual.

Section 4A2.3-3 Annuities--Incomplete Debt Claims

A. General

If a creditor agency sends OPM a notice of debt or an incomplete debt claim against an annuitant, OPM will not offset the annuity. OPM will notify the creditor agency that the procedures described in this part and 4 CFR 102.4 must be completed and SF 2805 or other acceptable claim form must be completed and sent to OPM.

No time limit will be given for the submission of a debt claim against an annuity; however, a complete debt claim must be received within 10 years of the date the Government's right to collect first accrued. (See 4 CFR 102.3(b)(3).)

Section 4A2.3-4 Annuities--Complete Debt Claims

A. General

1. **Notice**

    When OPM receives a complete debt claim and an application for annuity, OPM will:

    - Offset the annuity;

    - Pay the creditor agency; and

    - Mail the debtor a copy of the debt claim along with notice of the payment to the creditor agency.

2. **Beginning Deductions**

    - If OPM has already completed adjudication of the debtor's annuity payment, deductions will begin with the next available annuity payment.

    - If OPM is in the process of adjudicating the application for annuity, deductions will not be taken from interim annuity payments, but will begin with the first regular annuity payment after adjudication has been completed.

3. **Updating Accrued Interest**

    Once OPM has completed a collection, if there are additional accrued interest charges, the creditor agency must contact OPM regarding any additional amount due within 90 days of the date of the final payment.

B. Claims Held for Future Recovery

1. If OPM receives an application for annuity within 1 year of the date the agency's debt claim was received, the debt will be processed as stated in paragraph A of this section.

2. If OPM receives an application for annuity more than 1 year after the agency's debt claim was submitted:

    - OPM will contact the creditor agency to see if the debt is still outstanding.

Section 4A2.3-4 Annuities--Complete Debt Claims (Cont.)

B. Claims Held for Future Recovery (Cont.)

- If the debt is still due, the creditor agency should permit the debtor to offer a satisfactory repayment plan in lieu of offset if the debtor establishes that his or her changed financial circumstances would make the offset unjust. (See 4 CFR 102.4(c).)

- If the agency decides to pursue the offset, it must submit the requested information and any new instructions about the collection to OPM.

Debt Collection
Chapter 4

Subpart 4A2.4 Installment Withholdings

Section 4A2.4-1 Installment Withholdings

A. General	When possible, OPM will collect a creditor agency's claim in one payment from the debtor's refund or annuity.
B. Rule	If collection must be made from an annuity and the debt is large, the creditor agency must generally accept payment in installments. **The responsibility for establishing and notifying the debtor of the amount of the installments belongs to the creditor agency.** (See section 4A2.2-2, paragraph E).
C. Limitation on Installment Withholdings	OPM will not make an installment deduction for more than 50 percent of net annuity, unless:

- A higher percentage is needed to satisfy a judgment against a debtor within 3 years; or

- The annuitant has consented to the higher amount in writing.

NOTE: All correspondence concerning installment deductions received by OPM will be referred to the creditor agency for consideration.

CSRS Debt Collection Chapter 4 FERS

Subpart 4A2.5 Special Processing for Fraud Claims

Section 4A2.5-1 Special Processing for Fraud Claims

A. General

When an agency sends a claim indicating fraud, presentation of a false claim, misrepresentation by the debtor or any other party with an interest in the claim, or any claim based in whole or part on conduct violating the antitrust laws, to the Department of Justice (Justice) for possible treatment as a fraud claim (4 CFR 101.3), the following special procedures apply.

B. Agency Processing

If the debtor is separated or separates while Justice is reviewing the claim, the paying agency must send the SF 2806 or SF 3100 to OPM (see section 4A2.2-4, paragraph B). The agency where the claim arose must send OPM notice that a claim is pending with Justice. (See section 4A2.2-2, paragraph F, for instructions on giving OPM a notice of debt.)

C. Department of Justice Processing

1. The Attorney General or a designee will decide whether a debt claim sent in by an agency will be reserved for collection by Justice as a fraud claim. Upon receiving a possible fraud claim to be collected by offset from the Fund, the Attorney General or a designee must notify OPM. The notice to OPM must contain the following:

   - The name, date of birth, and Social Security number of the debtor;
   - The amount of the possible fraud claim, if known;
   - The basis of the possible fraud claim; and
   - A statement that the claim is being considered as a possible fraud claim, the collection of which is reserved to Justice.

2. When there is a pending refund application, the Attorney General or designee must:

   - File a complaint seeking a judgment on the claim and send a copy of the complaint to OPM;
   - Refer the claim to the agency where the claim arose and submit a copy of the referral to OPM within 180 days of the date of either the notice from the agency that a claim is pending with Justice (see paragraph B) or notice from Justice that it has received a possible fraud claim (see paragraph C1), whichever is earlier. (See 4 CFR 101.3.)

Section 4A2.5-1 Special Processing for Fraud Claims (Cont.)

D. **Agency Processing of a Claim Returned by the Department of Justice**

If the claim is returned to the agency where it arose for collection, the agency must:

- Begin administrative collection action in accordance with the provisions of 4 CFR 102.4; and

- Send an SF 2805 to OPM as required in section 4A2.2-2

E. **OPM Processing Against Refunds**

When OPM receives a notice described in paragraphs B or C1 above, it will take the following actions:

1. If the amount of the debt is known:

    - Notify the debtor it has received notice of a debt from the agency or the Department of Justice, as appropriate;

    - Notify the debtor that the amount of the debt will be held for at least 180 days from the date of the agency's or the Department of Justice's notice; and

    - Pay the balance, if any, to the debtor.

2. If the amount of the debt is not known:

    - Notify the debtor it has received notice of a debt in an undetermined amount to be offset from his or her lump-sum credit; and

    - Notify the debtor of the time limits for perfecting the Government's claim against his or her retirement benefits and the possible release of any balance that may be due as specified below.

3. If the amount of the debt is not known when OPM is notified of the existence of the debt, OPM will not release any payment to the debtor until:

    - The amount of the debt is established by the agency or the Department of Justice; or

    - There is a final decision in the court, if the Attorney General files a complaint and notifies OPM within the applicable 180-day period; or

Section 4A2.5-1 Special Processing for Fraud Claims (Cont.)

E. OPM Processing Against Refunds (Cont.)	• 180 days after the date of the agency's or the Department of Justice's notice to OPM, if a complaint is not filed and Justice does not notify OPM that the claim has been referred back to the creditor agency for collection; or • Within 120 days of OPM's notice to the creditor agency, if the Department of Justice notifies OPM that the claim has been returned to the creditor agency for collection. NOTE: The agency may request one extension of time of not more than 60 days. (See section 4A2.3-1, paragraph B.)
F. OPM Processing Against Annuities	If the debtor has filed an annuity claim, OPM will not take action against the annuity. OPM will continue to pay the annuity unless and until there is a final judgment for the United States or submission of a complete debt claim.
G. OPM Collection and Payment of the Debt	1. If the United States obtains a judgment against the debtor for the amount of the debt or the creditor agency submits a complete debt claim, OPM will pay the debt to the creditor agency as provided in subpart 4A2.3 and 4A2.4. 2. If the suit or the administrative proceeding results in a judgment for the debtor without establishing a debt to the United States, OPM will pay the balance of the refund to the debtor upon receipt of a certified copy of the judgment or administrative decision.

CSRS Court Orders FERS
Chapter 5

Table of Contents

Subchapter 5A CSRS and FERS

Part 5A1 General Information

Section 5A1.1-1 Overview 1
   A. Introduction 1
   B. Requests for Advice/Information 1
   C. Handbook for Attorneys 2
   D. Topics Covered 2
   E. Organization of Chapter 3
   F. Statement of Authority 3

Part 5A2 Garnishment Orders

Section 5A2.1-1 Definitions 4
   A. Child Support 4
   B. Alimony 4
   C. Disposable Annuity 4

Section 5A2.1-2 Garnishment Orders 6
   A. General Rule 6
   B. Restrictions on Amount to be Garnished 6
   C. Payments Under a Garnishment Order 6
   D. Where to File Garnishment Orders 7

Part 5A3 Child Abuse Judgment Enforcement Orders

Section 5A3.1-1 Definitions 8
   A. Child Abuse Judgment Enforcement Order 8
   B. Child Abuse Creditor 8
   C. Disposable Annuity 8

Section 5A3.1-2 Child Abuse Judgment Enforcement Orders 9
   A. General 9
   B. Payments Under Child Abuse Judgment Enforcement Orders 9
   C. Where to File Child Abuse Judgment Enforcement Orders 9

Part 5A4 Apportionment Orders

Section 5A4.1-1 Definitions 10
A. Self-Only Annuity 10
B. Gross Annuity 10
C. Net Annuity 10
D. Former Spouse 10

Section 5A4.1-2 Apportionment Orders 11
A. General Rule 11

Section 5A4.1-3 Preparing an Apportionment Order 12
A. Applicability of State Law 12
B. Which Courts Can Issue Order 12
C. Content of Order 12
D. Maximum Benefits Payable 12

Section 5A4.1-4 Filing an Apportionment Order 13
A. General 13
B. Application Must be in Writing 13
C. Information to Include in Application 13
D. Certification of Marital Status 14
E. OPM Address 14

Section 5A4.1-5 Miscellaneous 15
A. Health Benefits Coverage 15
B. Alternative Annuity Election 15

Part 5A5 Survivor Benefit Orders

Section 5A5.1-1 Definitions 16
A. Former Spouse 16
B. Former Spouse Survivor Annuity 16

Section 5A5.1-2 Survivor Benefit Orders 17
A. General 17
B. Which Courts Can Issue Order 17
C. Content of Order 17
D. Which Court Orders Can Award CSRS Survivor Benefits 17
E. Modification Restrictions 18
F. Maximum Benefits Payable 19
G. Filing the Order 19

CSRS Court Orders FERS
Chapter 5

Section 5A5.1-3 Miscellaneous 20
   A. Health Benefits Coverage 20
   B. Alternative Annuity Election 20

Part 5A6 Release of Information

Section 5A6.1-1 Orders for Release of Retirement and Insurance Records 21
   A. General 21
   B. Where to Serve When Individual Is No Longer an Employee 21
   C. Where to Serve When Individual Employed by Only One Agency
      With No Break in Service 21
   D. Where to Serve When Individual Employed by More Than One Agency
      or Has a Break in Service 21
   E. Information to Include in a Court Order 21
   F. OPM Address 22

Subchapter 5B Job Aid

Section 5B1.1-1 Order Form for Attorney's Handbook 23
Order Form for Attorney's Handbook 24

Appendix -- Model Language for Use in Court Orders 25

Introduction 25

000 Series--Special Technical Provisions 27
001 Language required in Qualified Domestic Relations Orders 27

**100 Series--Identification of the benefits and instructions that OPM pay the
     former spouse** 28
101 Identifying retirement benefits and directing OPM to pay the former
    spouse 28
111 Protecting a former spouse entitled to military retired pay 28

200 Series--Computing the amount of the former spouse's benefit 29
201 Award of a fixed monthly amount 29
202 Award of a percentage 29
203 Award of a fraction 29
204 Award of a prorata share 30
211 Award based on a stated formula 30
231 Awarding COLA's on fixed monthly amounts 31
232 Excluding COLA's on awards other than fixed monthly amounts 31

CSRS and FERS Handbook   April 1998

300 Series--Type of annuity 32
301 Awards based on benefits actually paid 32
311 Awards of earned annuity in cases where the actual annuity is based on disability ... 32

400 Series--Refunds of employee contributions 34
401 Barring payment of a refund of employee contributions 34
402 Dividing a refund of employee contributions 34

500 Series--Death of the former spouse 35
501 Full annuity restored to the retiree 35
502 Former spouse share paid to children 35
503 Former spouse share paid to the court 35

700 Series--Computing the amount of the former spouse's benefit 36
701 Award of the maximum survivor annuity 36
702 Award that continues the pre-divorce survivor annuity benefits 37
703 Award of a prorata share 37
704 Award of a fixed monthly amount 37
711 Award of a percentage or fraction of the employee annuity 38
712 Award based on a stated formula as a share of employee annuity 38
721 Award of a percentage or fraction of the maximum survivor annuity 38
722 Award based on a stated formula as a share of maximum survivor annuity 39
751 Changing amount of former spouse survivor annuity based on remarriage
    before retirement 39
752 Changing amount of former spouse survivor annuity based on remarriage
    after retirement 39

800 Series--Paying the cost of a former spouse survivor annuity 41
801 Costs to be paid from the employee annuity 41
802 Costs to be paid from former spouse's share of the employee annuity .. 41

900 Series--Refunds of employee contributions 42
901 Barring payment of a refund of employee contributions 42
902 Dividing a refund of employee contributions 42

CSRS Court Orders FERS
Chapter 5

Subchapter 5A CSRS and FERS
Part 5A1 General Information

Section 5A1.1-1 Overview

A. Introduction

Courts can issue orders that award benefits to legally separated spouses, former spouses, and children of current employees, former employees, and retirees under CSRS and FERS. Courts can also issue orders to collect amounts awarded in child abuse cases. The purpose of this Chapter is to provide agency personnel with general information about the different kinds of court orders and benefits that can be awarded, as well as guidance on how to respond to requests for information and assistance.

B. Requests for Advice/ Information

Agency personnel should **not** attempt to advise an employee, an employee's spouse, or an attorney on how to draft a court order to award CSRS or FERS benefits. This is the task of the attorneys involved. The requirements that must be satisfied for OPM to honor a court order are set out in the law and regulations cited in this Chapter.

NOTE: The appendix to this Chapter contains model language to use in court orders, and attorneys can purchase a Handbook for Attorneys (see paragraph C below).

An agency's efforts to advise individuals in legal matters involving domestic disputes can, despite good intentions, harm more than help. Instead, agency personnel should provide a copy of this Chapter to any individual seeking help in this area.

With regard to requests for an individual's records, agency personnel must consult Privacy Act rules and applicable regulations before disclosing the information. This may require that you consult with your agency's legal counsel. (See part 5A6 concerning court orders for retirement and insurance information.) Commonly requested information includes a statement of retirement system coverage, the amount of money to the employee's credit in the retirement fund, and an annuity estimate using the employee's service history to date. If an agency provides an annuity estimate, as agencies generally do for employees at or near retirement, it should clearly state that the benefit calculation is only an estimate, and is not binding on the Government. Agencies should not speculate about

Section 5A1.1-1 Overview (Cont.)

B.	Requests for Advice/ Information (Cont)	future promotions, program changes, or any other non-factual information, and should avoid giving annuity estimates for employees who are not near retirement. Official computations are made by OPM only at the time benefits become payable. It is **not** appropriate for agency personnel to attempt a "present value" computation of an employee's future benefits. Present value computations should be prepared by a qualified private actuary. Such computations of the total actuarial value of retirement benefits require application of various economic and mortality assumptions and are beyond the scope of an employing agency's or OPM's responsibility. Also, agencies should not attempt to determine the proper division of benefits between the employee and spouse.
C.	Handbook for Attorneys	Attorneys may want to order "A Handbook for Attorneys on Court-ordered Retirement, Health Benefits, and Life Insurance Under the Civil Service Retirement System, Federal Employees Retirement System, Federal Employees Health Benefits Program, and Federal Employees Group Life Insurance Program". An order form for local reproduction is included in Subchapter 5B. In addition to the printed text of the law and regulations, the Handbook includes extensive model paragraphs that can be used to draft orders that will meet OPM's requirements. Also included is a computer diskette containing the model language in several formats.
		The Handbook for Attorneys is also available on OPM Mainstreet, OPM's bulletin board system. > (See Chapter 1, Section 1B3.1-1 for instructions on downloading from the Bulletin Board.) < The telephone number is (202) 606-4800.
D.	Topics Covered	This Chapter covers the rules and procedures that govern: • Garnishment of Federal retirement benefits; • Apportionment of Federal retirement benefits; • Survivor benefit orders; and • Serving court orders on OPM and/or the employing agency. • Payments of amounts of Federal retirement benefits subject to child abuse judgment enforcement orders.

Section 5A1.1-1 Overview (Cont.)

E. **Organization of Chapter**

This Chapter has five parts.

Part	Name of Part	Page
5A1	General Information	1
5A2	Garnishment Orders	4
5A3	Child Abuse Judgment Enforcement Orders	8
5A4	Apportionment Orders	10
5A5	Survivor Benefit Orders	16
5A6	Release of Information	21

F. **Statement of Authority**

This Chapter and its contents are based on the laws and regulations cited below.

- United States Code: 5 U.S.C. 8341(h), 8342(j), 8345(j), and 8424(b); 5 U.S.C. 8445 and 8467; 42 U.S.C. 659 et seq.; 5 U.S.C. 8905(c)

- Code of Federal Regulations: 5 CFR Part 581; 5 CFR 831, Subparts A, Q, and T; 5 CFR 831.106; 5 CFR 841, Subparts A and I, and 5 CFR 841.108; 5 CFR 890, Subpart H

Part 5A2 Garnishment Orders

Section 5A2.1-1 Definitions

A. Child Support

"Child support" means periodic payments of funds for the support and maintenance of a child or children, and, subject to and in accordance with State or local law, includes, but is not limited to, payments to provide for health care, education, recreation, clothing, or to meet other specific needs of the child or children. The term also includes attorney's fees, interest, and court costs, if they are expressly made recoverable as child support under a decree, order, or judgment issued in accordance with applicable State or local law by a court of competent jurisdiction.

B. Alimony

"Alimony" means periodic payments of funds for the support and maintenance of a spouse or former spouse, and, subject to and in accordance with State or local law, includes, but is not limited to, separate maintenance, alimony **pendente lite**, maintenance, and spousal support. Alimony also includes attorney's fees, interest, and court costs, if they are expressly made recoverable as alimony under a decree, order, or judgment issued in accordance with applicable State or local law by a court of competent jurisdiction.

This term does not include any payments or transfer of property or its value by an individual to his or her spouse in compliance with any community property settlement, equitable distribution of property, or other division of property between spouses or former spouses.

NOTE: Attorney's fees, interest, and court costs, may be recovered only if they are considered alimony or child support under State or local law. OPM cannot comply with a garnishment order for payment of these items unless it expressly states that they constitute alimony or child support.

C. Disposable Annuity

"Disposable annuity" means the amount of annuity payable after deducting from the gross annuity any amounts that are--

- Owed by the retiree to the United States;

- Deducted for health benefits premiums;

- Deducted for basic life insurance premiums;

Section 5A2.1-1 Definitions (Cont.)

C. **Disposable Annuity (Cont.)**

- Deducted for Medicare premiums;

- Already payable to another person based on a court order acceptable for processing or a child abuse judgment enforcement order; and

- Properly withheld for Federal, State, or local income tax purposes, if the withholding of the amounts is authorized or required by law and if amounts withheld are not greater than would be the case if the individual claimed all dependents to which he or she was entitled. The withholding of additional amounts pursuant to 26 U.S.C. 3402(i) may be permitted only when the individual presents evidence of tax obligation that supports the additional withholding.

Section 5A2.1-2 Garnishment Orders

A. General Rule

Garnishment is a legal process for enforcing existing legal obligations. CSRS and FERS benefits can be garnished only for alimony or child support. The garnishment order must conform with all State law requirements for garnishment actions involving private employers.

Public Law 93-647 (effective January 1, 1975) and Public Law 95-30 (effective June 1, 1977) amended the Social Security Act (title 42, United States Code) to provide that the United States Government will comply with the terms of a valid court order for garnishment or attachment (or other legal process) of remuneration for employment where the order is based upon an obligation to provide alimony or child support. These are the same provisions that require agencies to comply with similar garnishment orders against employees' salaries.

The information provided in this section outlines the most important aspects of the requirements concerning apportionment orders. The governing regulations are found at 5 CFR Part 581, Garnishment Orders.

B. Restrictions on Amount to be Garnished

Public Law 95-30 sets up limitations on garnishments issued to enforce a support obligation.

1. An individual who has remarried and who is supporting his or her current spouse or a dependent child other than a child awarded support under the garnishment order may be garnished up to 50 percent of the disposable annuity, or 55 percent if the garnishment is for a support payment that is more than 3 months in arrears.

2. An individual who has not remarried, or is not supporting a dependent child other than a child awarded support under the garnishment order may be garnished up to 60 percent of the disposable annuity, or 65 percent if the garnishment is for a support payment that is more than 3 months in arrears.

C. Payments Under a Garnishment Order

OPM cannot vary its normal payment cycles to comply with a garnishment order. Garnishment payments are made on the first business day of the month for benefits that accrued during the previous month.

Section 5A2.1-2 Garnishment Orders (Cont.)

D. Where to File Garnishment Orders

Send garnishment orders for annuitants to OPM at the following address:

**Office of Personnel Management
Office of Retirement Programs
Court Order Benefit Section
Post Office Box 17
Washington, DC 20044**

For individuals still employed, send garnishment orders to the employing agency.

Part 5A3 Child Abuse Judgment Enforcement Orders

Section 5A3.1-1 Definitions

A. **Child Abuse Judgment Enforcement Order**	"Child abuse judgment enforcement order" means a court or administrative order requiring OPM to pay a portion of an employee's annuity or a refund of employee contributions to a child abuse creditor as a means of collecting a judgment rendered for physically, sexually, or emotionally abusing a child as defined in sections 8345(j)(3)(B) and 8467(c)(2) of title 5, United States Code.
B. **Child Abuse Creditor**	"Child abuse creditor" means an individual who applies for benefits under CSRS or FERS based on a child abuse judgment enforcement order.
C. **Disposable Annuity**	"Disposable annuity" means the amount of annuity payable after deducting from the gross annuity any amounts that are--

- Owed by the retiree to the United States;

- Deducted for health benefits premiums;

- Deducted for basic life insurance premiums;

- Deducted for Medicare premiums;

- Already payable to another person based on a court order acceptable for processing or a child abuse judgment enforcement order; and

- Properly withheld for Federal, State, or local income tax purposes, if the withholding of the amounts is authorized or required by law and if amounts withheld are not greater than would be the case if the individual claimed all dependents to which he or she was entitled. The withholding of additional amounts pursuant to 26 U.S.C. 3402(i) may be permitted only when the individual presents evidence of a tax obligation that supports the additional withholding.

Unless the court order expressly provides otherwise, net annuity also includes a lump-sum payment made to a retiree under section 8343a of title 5, U.S.C.

CSRS Court Orders FERS
Chapter 5

Section 5A3.1-2 Child Abuse Judgment Enforcement Orders

A. General	The Child Abuse Accountability Act (P.L. 103-358), signed October 14, 1994, requires OPM to comply with certain court orders for the enforcement of judgments rendered against employees or retirees for physical, sexual, or emotional abuse of a child. The Act applies to court orders OPM receives on or after October 14, 1994. OPM's regulations affect only benefits payable under CSRS and FERS, not the Thrift Savings Plan, which OPM does not administer. OPM will apply the procedure established in the regulations for garnishment orders found in 5 CFR Part 581, when processing child abuse judgment enforcement orders. The specific governing regulations are found at 5 CFR Part 838, Subpart K, Child Abuse Judgment Enforcement Orders.
B. Payments Under Child Abuse Judgment Enforcement Orders	OPM cannot vary its normal payment cycles to comply with a child abuse judgment enforcement order. Payments are made on the first business day of the month for benefits that accrued during the previous month.
C. Where to File Child Abuse Judgment Enforcement Orders	Send child abuse judgment enforcement orders against annuitants to OPM at the following address: Office of Personnel Management Office of Retirement Programs Court Order Benefit Section Post Office Box 17 Washington, DC > 20044-0017 < For judgments against individuals still employed, send orders to the employing agency.

Part 5A4 Apportionment Orders

Section 5A4.1-1 Definitions

A. Self-Only Annuity

"Self-only annuity" means the recurring unreduced payments to a retiree whose annuity is not being reduced to provide a survivor annuity to anyone.

B. Gross Annuity

"Gross annuity" means the amount of self-only annuity less any applicable survivor reduction, but before any deductions.

C. Net Annuity

"Net annuity" under CSRS means the amount of annuity payable after deducting from the gross annuity deductions for any amounts that are--

1. Owed by the retiree to the United States;

2. Deducted for health benefits premiums;

3. Deducted for life insurance premiums;

4. Deducted for Medicare premiums;

5. Already payable to another person based on a court order acceptable for processing or a child abuse judgment enforcement order; or

6. Properly withheld for Federal, State, or local income tax purposes, if amounts withheld are not greater than they would be if the individual claimed all dependents to which he or she was entitled. The withholding of additional amounts pursuant to 26 U.S.C. 3402(i) may be permitted only when the individual presents evidence of a tax obligation that supports the additional withholding.

NOTE: "Net annuity" under FERS refers to the amount of annuity payable after deducting from the gross annuity any amounts listed in 1 through 4 above, but before the Federal income tax deduction listed in 6.

D. Former Spouse

"Former spouse" means, in connection with a court order affecting employee retirement benefits, a living person whose marriage to an employee or retiree has been subject to a divorce, annulment, or legal separation resulting in a court order.

Section 5A4.1-2 Apportionment Orders

A. General Rule

Apportionment orders are orders that divide an employee's annuity or refund in accordance with a court order related to a divorce or legal separation.

Sections 8345(j) and 8467 of title 5, United States Code, authorizes OPM to comply with apportionment orders that meet certain specifications. In particular, the law requires OPM to apportion an annuity or refund in accordance with the express provisions of a qualifying order, decree, or property settlement. OPM is authorized to make payments directly to the former or separated spouse if the terms of the court order expressly provide for payment in such a manner.

The information provided in this section outlines the most important aspects of the requirements concerning apportionment orders. The governing regulations are found at 5 CFR Part 831, Subparts Q and T and 5 CFR Part 841, Subpart I.

Section 5A4.1-3 Preparing an Apportionment Order

A. Applicability of State Law	The division of an employee's, former employee's or retiree's annuity or contributions is governed by State law.
B. Which Courts Can Issue Order	For purposes of this section, "court" means any court of any State, the District of Columbia, the Commonwealth of Puerto Rico, Guam, the Northern Mariana Islands, or the Virgin Islands, and any Indian court.
C. Content of Order	The court order should specify exactly what it wants OPM to do. 1. The court order must expressly provide for payment of a portion of the employee's or retiree's monthly annuity (or contributions); and 2. The spouse's share must be stated as fixed amount, a percentage or a fraction of the annuity, or be expressed as a formula whose value is readily apparent from the face of the order or normal OPM files. 3. If the apportionment amount is derived using a formula, percentage, or fraction, the order must specify the type of annuity to which the formula, percentage, or fraction is to be applied--self-only, gross, or net. NOTE: Apportionment orders concerning CSRS and FERS are not subject to the Employee Retirement Income Security Act (ERISA). ERISA forms should not be used.
D. Maximum Benefits Payable	There is no percentage limitation on how much of a retirement annuity payment can be awarded to a former spouse. However, payment under a court order may not exceed: • The net annuity, in cases involving annuities; or • The amount of the lump-sum credit, in cases involving refunds of contributions.

Section 5A4.1-4 Filing an Apportionment Order

A. General

Before any benefits can be paid to the former spouse, the former spouse must:

- Submit a written request to OPM; and

- Provide proper documentation so that OPM can establish the validity of the court order.

- OPM's regulations on this subject are found at Appendix A through Q of Part 831--Guidelines for Interpreting State Court Orders Dividing Civil Service Retirement Benefits.

B. Application Must Be In Writing

A former spouse, personally or through a representative, must apply in writing to be eligible for a portion of the retiree's annuity. A special form is not required.

C. Information to Include in Application

The former spouse must include the following information in his or her letter of application:

- Full name;

- Mailing address;

- A certified copy of the court order granting benefits;

IMPORTANT: A certified copy is a copy of the order signed and certified by an official of the court that issued the order, verifying that it is a true copy of the original--usually by means of a seal or raised stamp and the official's signature or initials. A photocopy of a certified copy is not acceptable.

- A signed statement that the court order has not been amended, superseded, or set aside;

- Identifying information concerning the employee or retiree, including his or her full name, date of birth, civil service annuity (CSA) claim number if retired, and a Social Security number; and

- If the employee is not yet retired, his or her mailing address.

Section 5A4.1-4 Filing an Apportionment Order (Cont.)

D. Certification of

When payments are subject to termination upon remarriage, no payment

Marital Status	may be made until the former spouse submits, on a prescribed form, a statement to OPM that he or she:

- Has not remarried;

- Will notify OPM within 15 calendar days of the date of any remarriage; and

- Acknowledges personal liability for any overpayment to him or her resulting from a remarriage.

OPM may require recertification of these statements. |
| **E. OPM Address** | Send applications for court-awarded CSRS or FERS benefits and requests for information to:

    Office of Personnel Management
    Office of Retirement Programs
    Court Order Benefit Section
    Post Office Box 17
    Washington, DC > 20044-0017 < |

Section 5A4.1-5 Miscellaneous

A. **Health Benefits Coverage**

A former spouse who is awarded a portion of an employee's or retiree's CSRS or FERS annuity by a qualifying court order, regardless of whether that benefit is payable now or in the future, is eligible to enroll for health benefits coverage under the Federal Employees Health Benefits (FEHB) program under certain conditions. These conditions and other rules that apply to FEHB coverage of former spouses are covered in 5 CFR 890.801 et seq. and in the Federal Employees Health Benefits Handbook for Personnel and Payroll Offices (formerly FPM Supplement 890-1).

B. **Alternative Annuity Election**

An employee who, at time of retirement, has a former spouse who is entitled by court order to a portion of the employee's annuity, or to a survivor annuity, may not elect the alternative annuity, regardless of when the marriage ended.

Part 5A5 Survivor Benefit Orders

Section 5A5.1-1 Definitions

A. Former Spouse	In connection with a court order awarding a former spouse survivor annuity, "former spouse" means a living person who was married for at least 9 months to an employee or retiree who performed at least 18 months of civilian service creditable under CSRS or FERS, and whose marriage to the employee or retiree was terminated prior to the death of the employee or retiree.
B. Former Spouse Survivor Annuity	"Former spouse survivor annuity" means a recurring benefit that is payable after the employee's or retiree's death to a former spouse who has not remarried before becoming 55 years of age.

CSRS — Court Orders Chapter 5 — FERS

Section 5A5.1-2 Survivor Benefit Orders

A. General

1. The former spouse of a CSRS employee or retiree may be awarded a survivor annuity pursuant to a court order.

   NOTE: The former spouse of a separated CSRS employee entitled to a deferred annuity may be awarded survivor benefits. However, no former spouse survivor annuity benefits are payable unless the employee dies after becoming age 62 and filing an application for retirement benefits.

2. The former spouse of a FERS employee or retiree, or of a separated FERS employee with title to deferred annuity, may be awarded a survivor annuity and/or basic employee death benefit pursuant to a court order.

   NOTE: A court order that awards a FERS survivor annuity also awards a corresponding share of the basic employee death benefit unless the order expressly provides otherwise.

   For a detailed discussion of former spouse survivor benefits, see Chapter 74.

   OPM's regulations on this subject are found at Appendix B to Subpart Q of 5 CFR Part 831--Guidelines for Interpreting State Court Orders Awarding Survivor Annuity Benefits to Former Spouses.

B. Which Courts Can Issue Order

For purposes of this section, "court" means any court of any State, the District of Columbia, the Commonwealth of Puerto Rico, Guam, the Northern Mariana Islands, or the Virgin Islands, and any Indian court.

C. Content of Order

For purposes of awarding a former spouse survivor annuity, the court order must state the former spouse's entitlement to a survivor annuity or direct an employee or retiree to provide a former spouse survivor annuity.

D. Which Court Orders Can Award CSRS Survivor Benefits

For purposes of affecting or awarding a CSRS former spouse survivor annuity, a court order is not a qualifying court order whenever:

1. The marriage was terminated before May 7, 1985; or

2. The marriage was terminated on or after May 7, 1985, and:

Section 5A5.1-2 Survivor Benefit Orders (Cont.)

D. Which Court Orders Can Award CSRS Survivor Benefits (Cont.)

- The employee retired under CSRS before May 7, 1985; and

- The retiree did not elect to provide a current spouse annuity for that spouse on or before May 7, 1985.

NOTE: These restrictions do not apply to FERS.

E. Modification Restrictions

For purposes of awarding, increasing, reducing, or eliminating a former spouse survivor annuity, or explaining, interpreting, or clarifying a court order that awards, increases, reduces, or eliminates a former spouse survivor annuity, the court order must be:

1. The first order terminating the marital relationship between the retiree and the former spouse. This is the original written order that first ends the marriage; or

2. Issued on a day prior to the date of retirement or death of the employee.

NOTE 1: "The first order terminating the marital relationship" does **not** include--

- Any order that amends, explains, clarifies, or interprets the original written order regardless of the effective date of the order making the amendment, explanation, clarification, or interpretation; or

- Any order issued under reserve jurisdiction or any other orders issued subsequent to the original written order terminating the marriage that divide marital property (even though no division of marital property was made in the order terminating the marriage) regardless of the effective date of the order.

NOTE 2: "Issued" means actually filed with the clerk of the court, and does **not** mean the effective date of a retroactive court order that is effective prior to the date when actually filed with the clerk of the court (for example, an order issued **nunc pro tunc**).

Section 5A5.1-2 Survivor Benefit Orders (Cont.)

E. Modification Restrictions (Cont.)	NOTE 3:	"Date of retirement" means the later of: • The date that the employee files an application for retirement; or • The date that employee's annuity commences (that is, begins to accrue).
F. Maximum Benefits Payable		The maximum combined total of all current and former spouse survivor annuities (not including any benefits based on an election of an insurable interest annuity) payable based solely on the service of the employee or former employee equals 55 percent (or 50 percent if based on a separation under FERS or a separation under CSRS that occurred before October 11, 1962) of the rate of the self-only annuity that otherwise would have been paid to the employee or retiree.
G. Filing the Order		The requirements and procedures outlined in section 5A4.1-4 above apply to the submission of survivor benefit orders to OPM.

Section 5A5.1-3 Miscellaneous

A. Health Benefits Coverage

A former spouse who is awarded a survivor annuity under CSRS or FERS by a qualifying court order may be eligible to enroll for health benefits coverage under the FEHB program if he or she meets certain requirements. These conditions and other rules that apply to FEHB coverage of former spouses are covered in 5 CFR 890.801 et seq., and in the Federal Employees Health Benefits Handbook for Personnel and Payroll Offices (formerly FPM Supplement 890-1).

B. Alternative Annuity Election

An employee who, at the time of retirement, has a former spouse who is entitled by court order to a survivor annuity, or to a portion of the employee's annuity, may not elect the alternative annuity, regardless of when the marriage ended.

CSRS Court Orders FERS
Chapter 5

Part 5A6 Release of Information

Section 5A6.1-1 Orders for Release of Retirement and Insurance Records

A. General

Any agency or OPM may release information from retirement and insurance records in response to a court order or subpoena issued with the specific approval of a judge. > We will also release information on the basis of the individual's written consent. <

The proper place to submit the order is determined by whether the person has been separated from Federal service.

The information provided in this section outlines the most important aspects of the requirements concerning release of information in response to court order. OPM's regulations on this subject are found at 8312.106 (CSRS) and 8431.108 (FERS).

B. Where to Serve When Individual Is No Longer an Employee

If the individual about whom the information is sought is not a current Federal employee, the court order should be addressed to OPM at the address in Paragraph F.

C. Where to Serve When Individual Employed by Only One Agency With No Break in Service

If the individual is still an active Federal employee, and all of his or her Federal service has been continuous and with the same agency, the records are with that agency. Service must be made upon the individual's employing agency.

NOTE: Agencies may release information in response to court orders only in accordance with OPM regulations in Parts 294 and 297 of Title 5, Code of Federal Regulations, and agency procedures.

D. Where to Serve When Individual Employed by More Than One Agency or Has a Break in Service

If the individual is currently a Federal employee but has had a break in service or has worked for more than one agency, some of the records will be in OPM files, while others will be in the employing agency's files. In this situation both OPM and the agency must be served with an order. See paragraphs C and F.

E. Information to Include in a Court Order

It takes OPM approximately 30 days to respond to an order. Submissions must include the employee's or former employee's full name, date of birth and Social Security number, if available, or OPM will not be able to locate the records.

Section 5A6.1-1 Orders for Release of Retirement and Insurance Records (Cont.)

F. OPM Address A court order > or subpoena signed by a judge < for release of retirement and insurance records in OPM's possession should be submitted to the following address:

>
**Office of Personnel Management
Reconsideration and Appeal Division
1900 E Street NW., Room 3457
Washington, DC 20015**

A signed release from the individual that specifically details the records needed, should be submitted to the following address:

**Office of Personnel Management
P. O. Box 45
Boyers, PA 16017** <

Subchapter 5B Job Aid

Section 5B1.1-1

A. **Order Form for Attorney's Handbook**

This subchapter contains a copy of the order form for the Handbook for Attorneys on Court-ordered Retirement, Health Benefits, and Life Insurance Under CSRS, FERS, FEHB Program, and FEGLI Program, RI 38-116, for local reproduction.

Attorneys whose family law practice includes Federal (or postal) employees or retirees will be interested in a publication prepared by the United States Office of Personnel Management (OPM). "A Handbook for Attorneys on Court-ordered Retirement, Health Benefits, and Life Insurance under the Civil Service Retirement System, Federal Employees Retirement System, Federal Employees Health Benefits Program, and Federal Employees Group Life Insurance Program" contains the laws and regulations that apply to court orders in divorces and legal separations affecting benefits under these programs. Since ERISA rules do not apply to Federal employees and retirees, this handbook is a must for anyone who works with court orders involving this group.

The retirement regulations spell out in detail what constitutes a court order that OPM can accept for processing, and even include extensive model paragraphs that can be used to draft orders that will meet OPM's requirements. OPM urges attorneys to use these model paragraphs. The January 1995 update of the handbook also includes information about recent legislation that allows employees and retirees to assign their Federal Employees Group Life Insurance benefits.

In addition to the printed text of the law and regulations, the handbook includes a 3.5 inch diskette containing the model language in Wordperfect 5.1, Word, and generic word processing formats. The handbook is available from the Superintendent of Documents at a cost of $14.00 per copy. A copy of the order form is reproduced below.

Order Processing Code:
7612

Superintendent of Documents Publication Order Form

Charge your order.
It's easy!
To fax your orders (202) 512-2250
To phone your orders (202) 512-1800

☐**YES**, please send me _____ copies of the **Handbook For Attorneys on Court-Ordered Retirement, Health Benefits, and Life Insurance Under Civil Service Retirement System, Federal Employees Retirement System, Federal Employees Health Benefits Program and Federal Employees Group Life Insurance Program, RI 38-116, Revised Jan. 95,** S/N 006-000-01408-9 $14.00 each ($17.50 foreign).

The total cost of my order is $ _____ Price includes regular shipping and handling and is subject to change. International customers please add 25%.

Check method of payment
☐ Check payable to Superintendent Documents
☐ GPO Deposit Account ☐☐☐☐☐☐☐-☐
☐ VISA   ☐ MasterCard

_____
Company or personal name   (Please type or print)

☐☐☐☐☐☐☐☐☐☐☐☐☐☐☐☐☐☐☐☐
☐☐☐☐ (expiration date) **Thank you for your order!**

_____
Additional address/attention line

_____
Street address

_____
City, State, Zip code

_____
Authorizing signature

_____
Daytime phone including area code
1/95

**Mail To: Superintendent of Documents
P.O. Box 371954, Pittsburgh, PA 15250-7954**

_____
Purchase order number (optional)

For Local Reproduction

| CSRS | Court Orders
Chapter 5 | FERS |

Appendix -- Model Language for Use in Court Orders

Introduction

This appendix contains the model language that is contained in the appendix to OPM's regulations on court orders. OPM encourages attorneys to use this model language. By using the model language, courts will know that the court order will have the effect described in this appendix.

Paragraphs 001 through 599 concern court orders that attempt to divide employee annuity. The model language in these paragraphs does not award a benefit that is payable after the death of the employee. A separate, distinct award of a former spouse survivor annuity is necessary to award a former spouse a benefit that is payable after the death of the employee. A court order directed at an employee annuity should include five elements:

- Identification of the benefits;
- Instructions that OPM pay the former spouse;
- A method for computing the amount of the former spouse's benefit;
- Identification of the type of annuity to which to apply a fraction, percentage or formula; and
- Instructions on what OPM should do if the employee leaves Federal service before retirement and applies for a refund of employee contributions.

The court order may also include instructions for disposition of the former spouse's share if the former spouse dies before the employee.

Paragraphs 701 through 999 contain model language for awarding survivor annuities and contain some examples that award a survivor annuity, but do not award benefits payable to the former spouse during the lifetime of the employee. A former spouse survivor annuity is not a continuation of a former spouse's share of an employee annuity after the death of the employee. A former spouse's entitlement to a portion of an employee annuity cannot continue after the death of the employee. A court order that attempts to extend the former spouse's entitlement to a portion of an employee annuity past the death of the employee is not effective. A separate, distinct award of a portion of the employee annuity is necessary to award a former spouse a benefit during the lifetime of the employee.

Attorneys should exercise great care in preparing provisions concerning former spouse survivor annuities because sections 8341(h)(4) and 8445(d) of title 5, United States Code, prohibit OPM from accepting modifications after the retirement or death of the employee. (See section 838.806 concerning unacceptable modifications.) A court order awarding a former spouse survivor annuity should include four elements:

- Identification of the retirement system;
- Explicit award of the former spouse survivor annuity;
- Method for computing the amount of the former spouse's benefit; and
- Instructions on what OPM should do if the employee leaves Federal service before retirement and applies for a refund of employee contributions.

The model language uses the terms "former spouse" to identify the spouse who is receiving a former spouse's portion of an employee annuity and "employee" to identify the Federal employee whose employment was covered by the Civil Service Retirement System or the Federal Employees Retirement System. Obviously, in drafting an actual court order the appropriate terms, such as "Petitioner" and "Respondent," or the names of the parties should replace "former spouse" and "employee."

Similarly, except when the provision applies only to the basic employee death benefit (defined in section 843.103 of this chapter) that is available only under the Federal Employees Retirement System, the models are drafted for employees covered by the Civil Service Retirement System (5 U.S.C. 8331 et seq.). The name of the retirement system should be changed for employees covered by the Federal Employees Retirement System (5 U.S.C. chapter 84). Statutory references used in the models are to CSRS provisions (such as 8341(h) of title 5, United States Code). When appropriate, the corresponding FERS provision (such as section 8445 of title 5, United States Code) should be used.

CSRS   Court Orders   **FERS**
Chapter 5

000 Series--Special Technical Provisions

001 Language required in Qualified Domestic Relations Orders

Using the following paragraph will expressly state that the provisions of the court order concerning CSRS or FERS benefits are governed by this part. A court order directed at employee annuity (or awarding a survivor annuity) that is labelled a "Qualified Domestic Relations Order" or is issued on an ERISA form will not be automatically rendered unacceptable under § 838.302(a) or § 838.803(a) if the court order contains the following paragraph.

"The court has considered the requirements and standard terminology provided in part 838 of Title 5, Code of Federal Regulations. The terminology used in the provisions of this order that concern benefits under the Civil Service Retirement System are governed by the standard conventions established in that part."

100 Series--Identification of the benefits and instructions that OPM pay the former spouse

101 Identifying retirement benefits and directing OPM to pay the former spouse	Using the following paragraph will expressly divide employee annuity to satisfy the requirements of § 838.303 and direct OPM to pay the former spouse a share of an employee annuity to satisfy the requirements of § 838.304. "[Employee] is (or will be) eligible for retirement benefits under the Civil Service Retirement System based on employment with the United States Government. [Insert language for computing the former spouse's share from 200 series of this appendix.] The United States Office of Personnel Management is directed to pay [former spouse]'s share directly to [former spouse]."
111 Protecting a former spouse entitled to military retired pay	Using the following paragraph will protect the former spouse interest in military retired pay in the event that the employee waives the military retired pay to allow crediting the military service under CSRS or FERS. The paragraph should be used only if the former spouse is awarded a portion of the military retired pay. "If [Employee] waives military retired pay to credit military service under the Civil Service Retirement System, [insert language for computing the former spouse's share from 200 series of this appendix.]. The United States Office of Personnel Management is directed to pay [former spouse]'s share directly to [former spouse]."

200 Series--Computing the amount of the former spouse's benefit

Paragraphs 201 through 204 contain model language for the most common types of awards that court orders make to former spouses. Subsequent paragraphs in the 200 series contain model language for less common, more complex awards.

Awards other than fixed amounts require that the court order specify the type of annuity ("gross," "net," or self-only) on which the award is computed. The types of annuity are defined in § 838.103. Variations on type of annuity are covered by the 300 series of this appendix.

201	**Award of a fixed monthly amount**	Using the following paragraph will award the former spouse a fixed monthly amount. OPM will not apply COLA's to a fixed monthly amount unless the court order expressly directs that OPM add COLA's using the language in paragraph 231 of this appendix or similar language. "[Employee] is (or will be) eligible for retirement benefits under the Civil Service Retirement System based on employment with the United States Government. [Former spouse] is entitled to $[insert a number] per month from [employee]'s civil service retirement benefits. The United States Office of Personnel Management is directed to pay [former spouse]'s share directly to [former spouse]."
202	**Award of a percentage**	Using the following paragraph will award the former spouse a stated percentage of the employee annuity. Unless the court order expressly directs that OPM not add COLA's to the former spouse's share of the employee annuity, OPM will add COLA's to keep the former spouse's share at the stated percentage. Paragraph 232 of this appendix provides language for excluding COLA's. "[Employee] is (or will be) eligible for retirement benefits under the Civil Service Retirement System based on employment with the United States Government. [Former spouse] is entitled to [insert a number] percent of [employee]'s [insert "gross," "net," or "self-only"] monthly annuity under the Civil Service Retirement System. The United States Office of Personnel Management is directed to pay [former spouse]'s share directly to [former spouse]."
203	**Award of a fraction**	Using the following paragraph will award the former spouse a stated fraction of the employee annuity. Unless the court order expressly directs that OPM not add COLA's to the former spouse's share of the employee annuity, OPM will add COLA's to keep the former spouse's share at the stated percentage. Paragraph 232 of this appendix provides language for excluding COLA's.

203	Award of a fraction (cont.)	"[Employee] is (or will be) eligible for retirement benefits under the Civil Service Retirement System based on employment with the United States Government. [Former spouse] is entitled to [insert fraction]ths of [employee]'s [insert "gross," "net," or "self-only"] monthly annuity under the Civil Service Retirement System. The United States Office of Personnel Management is directed to pay [former spouse]'s share directly to [former spouse]."
204	Award of a prorata share	Using the following paragraph will award the former spouse a prorata share of the employee annuity. Prorata share is defined in § 838.621. To award a prorata share the court order must state the date of the marriage. Unless the court order specifies a different ending date, the marriage ends for computation purposes on the date that the court order is filed with the court clerk. Unless the court order expressly directs that OPM not add COLA's to the former spouse's share of the employee annuity, OPM will add COLA's to keep the former spouse's share at the stated percentage. Paragraph 232 of this appendix provides language for excluding COLA's. "[Employee] is (or will be) eligible for retirement benefits under the Civil Service Retirement System based on employment with the United States Government. [Former spouse] is entitled to a prorata share of [employee]'s [insert "gross," "net," or self-only] monthly annuity under the Civil Service Retirement System. The marriage began on [insert date]. The United States Office of Personnel Management is directed to pay [former spouse]'s share directly to [former spouse]."
211	Award based on a stated formula	Using the following paragraphs will award the former spouse a share of the employee annuity based on a formula stated in the court order. The formula must be stated in the court order (including a court-approved property settlement agreement). The formula may not be incorporated by reference to a statutory provision or a court decision in another case. If the court order uses a formula, the court order must include any data that is necessary for OPM to apply the formula unless the necessary data is contained in normal OPM files. "[Employee] is (or will be) eligible for retirement benefits under the Civil Service Retirement System based on employment with the United States Government. [Former spouse] is entitled to a share of [employee]'s [insert "gross," "net," or self-only] monthly annuity under the Civil Service Retirement System to be computed as follows: "[Insert formula for computing the former spouse's share.] "The United States Office of Personnel Management is directed to pay [former spouse]'s share directly to [former spouse]."

Court Orders
Chapter 5

231 Awarding COLA's on fixed monthly amounts

Using the following paragraph will award COLA's in addition to a fixed monthly amount to the former spouse. The model awards COLA's at the same rate applied to the employee annuity.

> "[Employee] is (or will be) eligible for retirement benefits under the Civil Service Retirement System based on employment with the United States Government. [Former spouse] is entitled to $[insert a number] per month from [employee]'s civil service retirement benefits. When COLA's are applied to [employee]'s retirement benefits, the same COLA applies to [former spouse]'s share. The United States Office of Personnel Management is directed to pay [former spouse]'s share directly to [former spouse]."

232 Excluding COLA's on awards other than fixed monthly amounts

Using the following paragraph will prevent application of COLA's to a former spouse's share of an employee annuity in cases where the former spouse has been awarded a percentage, fraction or prorata share of the employee annuity, rather than a fixed dollar amount.

> "[Employee] is (or will be) eligible for retirement benefits under the Civil Service Retirement System based on employment with the United States Government. [Insert language for computing the former spouse's share from paragraph 202, 203, 204, or 211 of this appendix.] The United States Office of Personnel Management is directed to determine the amount of [former spouse]'s share on the date [insert "when [employee] retires" if the employee has not retired, or "of this order" if the employee is already retired] and not to apply COLA's to that amount. The United States Office of Personnel Management is directed to pay [former spouse]'s share directly to [former spouse]."

300 Series--Type of annuity

Awards of employee annuity to a former spouse (other than awards of fixed dollar amounts) must specify whether OPM will use the "gross," "net," or self-only annuity as defined in § 838.103 in determining the amount of the former spouse's entitlement. The court order may contain a formula that has the effect of creating other types of annuity, but the court order may only do this by providing a formula that starts from "gross," "net," or self-only annuity as defined in § 838.103.

301 Awards based on benefits actually paid	The court order may include a formula that effectively uses the court's definition of net annuity rather than the one provided by § 838.103. For example, using the following paragraph will award the former spouse a prorata share of the employee annuity reduced only by the amount deducted as premiums for basic life insurance under the Federal Employee Group Life Insurance Program.

> "[Employee] is (or will be) eligible for retirement benefits under the Civil Service Retirement System based on employment with the United States Government. [Former spouse] is entitled to a prorata share of [employee]'s monthly annuity under the Civil Service Retirement System, where monthly annuity means the self-only annuity less the amount deducted as premiums for basic life insurance under the Federal Employee Group Life Insurance Program. The marriage began on [insert date]. The United States Office of Personnel Management is directed to pay [former spouse]'s share directly to [former spouse]."

311 Awards of earned annuity in cases where the actual annuity is based on disability	Using the following paragraph will award a former spouse a prorata share of what the employee annuity would have been based on only the employee's actual service in cases where the actual employee annuity is based on disability. The paragraph also allows the court order to provide for the former spouse's share to begin when the employee reaches a stated age, using age 62 as an example. As with all other formulas the court order must specify whether the computation applies to "gross," "net," or self-only annuity. OPM will apply COLA's that occurred after the date of the disability retirement to the former spouse's share. The following paragraph should be used only for disability retirees under CSRS. Under FERS, section 8452 of title 5, United States Code, provides a formula for recomputation of disability annuities at age 62 to approximate an earned annuity. Therefore to award a portion of the "earned" benefit under FERS add the introductory phrase, "Starting when [employee] reaches age 62," to the paragraph describing how to compute the amount.

311 Awards of earned annuity in cases where the actual annuity is based on disability (cont.)	"[Employee] is (or will be) eligible for retirement benefits under the Civil Service Retirement System based on employment with the United States Government. Starting when [employee] reaches age 62, [former spouse] is entitled to a prorata share of [employee]'s [insert "gross," "net," or self-only] monthly annuity under the Civil Service Retirement System, where monthly annuity means the amount of [employee]'s monthly annuity computed as though [employee] had retired on an immediate, nondisability annuity on the commencing date of [employee]'s annuity based on disability. In computing the amount of the immediate annuity, the United States Office of Personnel Management will deem [employee] to have been age 62 at the time that [employee] retired on disability. The marriage began on [insert date]. The United States Office of Personnel Management is directed to pay [former spouse]'s share directly to [former spouse]."

400 Series--Refunds of employee contributions

Court orders that award a former spouse a portion of a future employee annuity of an employee who is not then eligible to retire should include an additional paragraph containing instructions that tell OPM what to do if the employee separates before becoming eligible to retire and requests a refund of employee contributions. The court order may award the former spouse a portion of the refund of employee contributions or bar payment of the refund of employee contributions.

401	**Barring payment of a refund of employee contributions**	Using the following paragraph will bar payment of the refund of employee contributions if payment of the refund of employee contributions would extinguish the former spouse's entitlement to a portion of the employee annuity.

> "The United States Office of Personnel Management is directed not to pay [employee] a refund of employee contributions."

402	**Dividing a refund of employee contributions**	Using the following paragraph will allow the refund of employee contributions to be paid but will award a prorata share of the refund of employee contributions to the former spouse. The sentence on the beginning date of the marriage is unnecessary if the beginning is stated elsewhere in the order. The award of a prorata share is used only as an example; the court order could provide another fraction, percentage, or formula, or a fixed amount. Note that a refund of employee contributions voids the employee's rights to an employee annuity and the former spouse's right to any portion of that annuity.

> "If [employee] becomes eligible and applies for a refund of employee contributions, [former spouse] is entitled to a prorata share of the refund of employee contributions. The marriage began on [insert date]. The United States Office of Personnel Management is directed to pay [former spouse]'s share directly to [former spouse]."

CSRS   **Court Orders**   **FERS**
Chapter 5

500 Series--Death of the former spouse

501 Full annuity restored to the retiree

No special provision is necessary to restore the entire annuity to the retiree upon the death of the former spouse. Unless the court order expressly provides otherwise, OPM will pay the former spouse's share to the retiree after the death of the former spouse.

502 Former spouse share paid to children

Using the following paragraph will award the former spouse's share of an employee annuity to the children, including any adopted children, of the employee and former spouse.

> "If [former spouse] dies before [employee], the United States Office of Personnel Management is directed to pay [former spouse]'s share of [employee]'s civil service retirement benefits to surviving children of the marriage including any adopted children, in equal shares. Upon the death of any child, that child's share will be distributed among the other surviving children."

The language may be modified to terminate the payments to the children when they reach a stated age. A court order that includes such a provision for termination must include sufficient information (such as the children's dates of birth) to permit OPM to determine when the children's interest terminates. OPM will not consider evidence outside the court order (and normal OPM files) to establish the children's dates of birth.

503 Former spouse share paid to the court

Using the following paragraph will provide for payment of the former spouse's share of an employee annuity to the court after the death of the former spouse. This would allow a court officer to administer the funds. "If [former spouse] dies before [employee], the United States Office of Personnel Management is directed to pay [former spouse]'s share of [employee]'s civil service retirement benefits to this court at the following address: "[Insert address where checks should be sent. The address may be up to six lines and should include sufficient information for court officials to credit the correct account.]"

700 Series--Computing the amount of the former spouse's benefit

Paragraphs 701 through 704 contain model language for awards of former spouse survivor annuities in amounts that do not require specification of the base on which the former spouse's share will be computed. Situations in which the computational base need not be specified include amounts defined by law or regulation. For example, the maximum former spouse survivor annuity is fixed by statute generally at 55 percent of the employee annuity under CSRS and 50 percent of the employee annuity under FERS.

Paragraphs 711 and 712 contain model language for awards of former spouse survivor annuities that use the employee annuity as the base on which the portion awarded will be computed (that is, on which percentage, fraction or formula will be applied). Paragraphs 721 and 722 contain model language for awards of former spouse survivor annuities that use the maximum possible survivor annuity as the base on which the portion awarded will be computed (that is, on which percentage, fraction or formula will be applied). Using the maximum possible survivor annuity as the base will generally award 55 percent under CSRS and 50 percent under FERS of the amount that using the employee annuity as the base would produce. Paragraphs 750 and higher contain model language to implement the most common other types of awards.

Each model paragraph includes a reference to the statutory provision under CSRS that authorizes OPM to honor court orders awarding former spouse survivor annuities. The FERS statutory provision that corresponds to section 8341(h) (mentioned in the first sentence of each example) is section 8445.

701 Award of the maximum survivor annuity	For a spouse who was married to a retiree at the time of retirement and consented to an election of less than a full survivor annuity, the maximum is the amount elected at retirement. For a spouse acquired after retirement and for whom the retiree elected less than the maximum survivor benefit, this language should be used only if the intent is to increase the survivor benefit to the maximum.
	Using the following paragraph will award the maximum possible former spouse survivor annuity. Under CSRS, the maximum possible survivor annuity is 55 percent of the employee annuity unless the surviving spouse or former spouse was married to the retiree at retirement and agreed to a lesser amount at that time. Under FERS, the maximum possible survivor annuity is 50 percent of the employee annuity unless the surviving spouse or former spouse was married to the retiree at retirement and agreed to a lesser amount at that time.
	"Under section 8341(h)(1) of title 5, United States Code, [former spouse] is awarded the maximum possible former spouse survivor annuity under the Civil Service Retirement System."

702 Award that continues the pre-divorce survivor annuity benefits

If a survivor benefit election of less than the full amount is in effect at the time of divorce, use of this language will emphasize that the lower benefit will remain in effect after the divorce. In all other instances this language will produce the maximum survivor annuity.

Using the following paragraph will award a former spouse survivor annuity equal to the amount that the former spouse would have received if the marriage were never terminated by divorce.

> "Under section 8341(h)(1) of title 5, United States Code, [Former spouse] is awarded a former spouse survivor annuity under the Civil Service Retirement System in the same amount to which [former spouse] would have been entitled if the divorce had not occurred."

703 Award of a prorata share

Using the following paragraph will award the former spouse a prorata share of the maximum possible survivor annuity. Prorata share is defined in § 838.922. To award a prorata share the court order must state the date of the marriage. Unless the court order specifies a different ending date, the marriage ends for computation purposes on the date that the court order is filed with the court clerk.

> "Under section 8341(h)(1) of title 5, United States Code, [former spouse] is awarded a former spouse survivor annuity under the Civil Service Retirement System. The amount of the former spouse survivor annuity will be equal to a prorata share. The marriage began on [insert date]."

704 Award of a fixed monthly amount

Using the following paragraph will award a former spouse survivor annuity that will start at the amount stated in the order when the employee or retiree dies, unless the stated amount exceeds the maximum possible former spouse survivor annuity. If the amount stated in the order exceeds the maximum possible former spouse survivor annuity, the court order will be treated as awarding the maximum. After payment of the former spouse survivor annuity has begun, COLA's will be applied in accordance with § 838.735. If the final sentence of this model paragraph is omitted, OPM will add COLA's occurring after the date of the employee's retirement or the date of issuance of the court order, whichever is later.

> "Under section 8341(h)(1) of title 5, United States Code, [former spouse] is awarded a former spouse survivor annuity under the Civil Service Retirement System. The amount of the former spouse survivor annuity will be equal to $[insert a number] per month. The Office of Personnel Management is ordered not to increase this amount by COLA's occurring before death of [employee or retiree]."

711 **Award of a percentage or fraction of the employee annuity**	Using the following paragraph will award a former spouse survivor annuity equal to the stated percentage or fraction of the employee annuity. The stated percentage or fraction may not exceed 55 percent under CSRS or 50 percent under FERS. "Under section 8341(h)(1) of title 5, United States Code, [former spouse] is awarded a former spouse survivor annuity under the Civil Service Retirement System. The amount of the former spouse survivor annuity will be equal to [insert a percentage or fraction] percent of the [employee]'s employee annuity."
712 **Award based on a stated formula as a share of employee annuity**	Using the following paragraphs will award a former spouse survivor annuity in an amount to be determined by applying a stated formula to employee annuity. The amount of the former spouse survivor annuity may not exceed 55 percent of the employee annuity under CSRS or 50 percent under FERS. The formula must be stated in the court order (including a court-approved property settlement agreement). The formula may not be incorporated by reference to a statutory provision or a court decision in another case. If the court order uses a formula, the court order must include any data that is necessary for OPM to evaluate the formula unless the necessary data is contained in normal OPM files. "Under section 8341(h)(1) of title 5, United States Code, [former spouse] is awarded a former spouse survivor annuity under the Civil Service Retirement System. The amount of the former spouse survivor annuity will be the portion of the [employee]'s employee annuity computed as follows: "[Insert formula.]"
721 **Award of a percentage or fraction of the maximum survivor annuity**	Using the following paragraph will award a former spouse survivor annuity equal to the stated percentage or fraction of the maximum possible survivor annuity. The stated percentage or fraction may not exceed 100 percent. "Under section 8341(h)(1) of title 5, United States Code, [former spouse] is awarded a former spouse survivor annuity under the Civil Service Retirement System. The amount of the former spouse survivor annuity will be equal to [insert a percentage or fraction] of the maximum possible survivor annuity.

CSRS   Court Orders   FERS
Chapter 5

722 Award based on a stated formula as a share of maximum survivor annuity

Using the following paragraphs will award a former spouse survivor annuity based on a stated formula to be applied to the maximum possible survivor annuity. The formula must be stated in the court order (including a court-approved property settlement agreement). The formula may not be incorporated by reference to a statutory provision or a court decision in another case. If the court order uses a formula, the court order must include any data that is necessary for OPM to evaluate the formula unless the necessary data is contained in normal OPM files.

> "Under section 8341(h)(1) of title 5, United States Code, [former spouse] is awarded a former spouse survivor annuity under the Civil Service Retirement System. The amount of the former spouse survivor annuity will be the portion of the maximum possible survivor annuity computed as follows:
>
> "[Insert formula.]"

751 Changing amount of former spouse survivor annuity based on remarriage before retirement

Using the following paragraph will award the maximum possible former spouse survivor annuity unless the employee remarries before retirement. Upon the employee's remarriage before retirement the amount of the former spouse survivor annuity changes to a prorata share. The maximum possible and prorata share are used as examples only; other amounts may be substituted. Similar language is not acceptable for remarriages after retirement.

> "Under section 8341(h)(1) of title 5, United States Code, [former spouse] is awarded the maximum possible former spouse survivor annuity under the Civil Service Retirement System unless [employee] remarries before retirement. If [employee] remarries before retirement, under section 8341(h)(1) of title 5, United States Code, [former spouse] is awarded a former spouse survivor annuity under the Civil Service Retirement System. The amount of the former spouse survivor annuity will be equal to a prorata share. The marriage to [former spouse] began on [insert date]."

752 Changing amount of former spouse survivor annuity based on remarriage after retirement

Using the following paragraph will award the maximum possible former spouse survivor annuity unless the employee remarries after retirement and elects to provide a survivor annuity for the spouse acquired after retirement. Upon the employee's remarriage after retirement and election to provide a survivor annuity for the spouse acquired after retirement, the amount of the former spouse survivor annuity changes to a prorata share. The maximum possible and prorata share are used as examples only; other amounts may be substituted. The change in the of the former spouse survivor annuity must be triggered by the election, which is a part of normal OPM files, rather than the remarriage, which is not documented in normal OPM files.

CSRS and FERS Handbook   Update 14   August 15, 1995

"Under section 8341(h)(1) of title 5, United States Code, [former spouse] is awarded the maximum possible former spouse survivor annuity under the Civil Service Retirement System unless [employee] elects to provide a survivor annuity for a new spouse acquired after retirement. If [employee] elects to provide a survivor annuity to a new spouse acquired after retirement, under section 8341(h)(1) of title 5, United States Code, [former spouse] is awarded a former spouse survivor annuity under the Civil Service Retirement System. The amount of the former spouse survivor annuity will be equal to a prorata share. The marriage to [former spouse] began on [insert date]."

CSRS   Court Orders   FERS
Chapter 5

800 Series--Paying the cost of a former spouse survivor annuity

A court order awarding a former spouse survivor annuity requires that the employee annuity be reduced. The reduction lowers the gross employee annuity. The costs associated with providing the former spouse survivor annuity must be paid by annuity reduction. Under § 838.807, if the former spouse is awarded a portion of the employee annuity sufficient to pay the cost associated with providing the survivor annuity, the former spouse's share may be reduced to pay the cost.

801	**Costs to be paid from the employee annuity**	No special provision on payment of the costs associated with providing the former spouse survivor annuity is necessary if the court intends the cost to be taken from the employee annuity.
802	**Costs to be paid from former spouse's share of the employee annuity**	Using the following paragraph will award the former spouse a prorata share of the employee annuity and a prorata share of the maximum possible survivor annuity and provide that the cost associated with the survivor annuity be deducted from the former spouses's share of the employee annuity. Prorata share and self-only annuity are used as examples only; another amount or type of annuity may be substituted.

> "[Employee] is (or will be) eligible for retirement benefits under the Civil Service Retirement System based on employment with the United States Government. [Former spouse] is entitled to a prorata share of [employee]'s self-only monthly annuity under the Civil Service Retirement System. [Former spouse]'s share of [employee]'s employee annuity will be reduced by the amount of the costs associated with providing the former spouse survivor annuity awarded in the next paragraph. The marriage began on [insert date]. The United States Office of Personnel Management is directed to pay [former spouse]'s share directly to [former spouse]."

> "Under section 8341(h)(1) of title 5, United States Code, [former spouse] is awarded a former spouse survivor annuity under the Civil Service Retirement System. The amount of the former spouse survivor annuity will be equal to a prorata share."

900 Series--Refunds of employee contributions

Court orders that award a former spouse survivor annuity based on the service of an employee who is not then eligible to retire should include an additional paragraph containing instructions that tell OPM what to do if the employee requests a refund of employee contributions before becoming eligible to retire. The court order may award the former spouse a portion of the refund of employee contributions or bar payment of the refund of employee contributions.

901	**Barring payment of a refund of employee contributions**	Using the following paragraph will bar payment of the refund of employee contributions if payment of the refund of employee contributions would extinguish the former spouse's entitlement to a former spouse survivor annuity.

> "The United States Office of Personnel Management is directed not to pay [employee] a refund of employee contributions."

902	**Dividing a refund of employee contributions**	Using the following paragraph will allow the refund of employee contributions to be paid but will award a prorata share of the refund of employee contributions to the former spouse. The award of a prorata share is used only an example; the court order could provide another fraction, percentage, or formula, or a fixed amount. A refund of employee contributions voids the employee's rights to an employee annuity unless the employee is reemployed under the retirement system. Payment of the refund of employee contributions will also extinguish the former spouse's right to a court-ordered portion of an employee annuity or a former spouse survivor annuity unless the employee is reemployed and reestablishes title to annuity benefits.

> "If [employee] becomes eligible and applies for a refund of employee contributions, [former spouse] is entitled to a prorata share of the refund of employee contributions. The marriage began on [insert date]. The United States Office of Personnel Management is directed to pay [former spouse]'s share directly to [former spouse]."

www.ingramcontent.com/pod-product-compliance
Lightning Source LLC
Chambersburg PA
CBHW062354220526
45472CB00008B/1802